GOING AFTER THE GOOD FRUIT

God's Character: The Fruit of the Spirit

WENDI MOEN

Foreword by MARIO MURILLO

PRESS

Going After The Good Fruit
God's Character: The Fruit of the Spirit
by Wendi Moen

Printed in the United States of America.

ISBN 9781498433457

Unless otherwise indicated, Scripture quotations are taken from the NEW AMERICAN STANDARD BIBLE®, Copyright © 1960,1962,1963,1968,1971,1972,1973,1975,1977,1995 by The Lockman Foundation. Used by permission.

Unless otherwise indicated, Scripture quotations are taken from the New Revised Standard Version Bible, copyright © 1989, Division of Christian Education of the National Council of the Churches of Christ in the United States of America. Used by permission. All rights reserved.

Unless otherwise indicated, Scripture quotations are taken from the *Holy Bible*, New Living Translation, copyright © 1996. Used by permission of Tyndale House Publishers, Inc. Wheaton, Illinois 60189. All rights reserved.

Unless otherwise indicated, Scripture quotations are taken from the Amplified® Bible, Copyright © 1954, 1958, 1962, 1964, 1965, 1987 by The Lockman Foundation Used by permission.

Unless otherwise indicated, Scripture quotations are taken from the HOLY BIBLE, NEW INTERNATIONAL VERSION ©. Copyright © 1973, 1978, 1984 International Bible Society. Used by permission of Zondervan. All rights reserved.

Greek words referenced throughout this book are from *Strong's Concordance* with Hebrew and Greek Lexicon at http://www.eliyah.com/lexicon.html.

Quotes in Chapter Seven are taken from http://www.wisdomquotes.com/002500.html and http://www.quotegarden.com/kindness.html.

Editorial assistance provided by Karen Roberts, RQuest, LLC.

Contact the author with questions or for permission to quote:

Wendi Moen
wendimoen7@gmail.com
pastorwendi@rrcf.net
www.wendimoen.com

www.xulonpress.com

Endorsements

"Wendi Moen beautifully illustrates the process of attaining the fruit of the Spirit. Pastor Wendi's aggressive approach to fruit is warmly and beautifully portrayed in her story about standing on her horse, China Doll. Wendi's own personal and forceful approach to manifesting the fruit of the Spirit is inspiring and thought provoking. Fruit doesn't just happen! Her unyielding desire to manifest the character of Jesus Christ fuels a hunger to attain the fruit of the Spirit. Her delightful writing style and years of wisdom captivate and depict the necessity of the fruit in every believer's life. She leads by example and discloses her own vulnerability and personal struggles. This book illustrates a fresh, new approach to attaining and living with the beautiful, delicious, loving, and fulfilling fruit of the Spirit."

Rev. Deborah Cofer
President, Streams in the Desert International, Inc.
Tarpon Springs, FL, USA

"This book is filled with the grace of God. It is a must-read for those longing to know His nature. Manifesting good fruit will enable us to be able to be trusted with His great gifts. I recommend this book by Wendi if you're longing to know Jesus and be more like Him."

Todd Bentley, Revivalist
President, Fresh Fire Ministries
Pineville, NC, USA

"This book is a must-read for those who want to have the right foundations and priorities for a fulfilled and influential Christian life. Wendi Moen brilliantly unpacks each fruit through sharing her own experiences (which you will relate to!) and through great revelatory insight into how to increasingly experience these marvelous fruits in your life."

Steve Backlund
Bethel Church and Igniting Hope Ministries
Redding, CA, USA

"You are in for a close, viable, connected look at God's love through fruit of His Spirit. This book really is written so well, and it is so good to see things personalized and prayerfully written! Wendi has revealed to you a very tangible tool (Time to Pray) and personal resource (Time to Apply). Through them you will see God's own heart and you will see it clearly and know it manifested in your own life! God's goodness to all! I have learned newness of God by reading it!"

Ila J. Henkel
Business Woman
Mesquite, NV, USA

"You, like me, may think that every possible insight about fruit of the Spirit is out there. Believe me, think again! Wendi has written a humorous, delightful, yet powerful argument for pursuing fruit in your life. She has given clarity, addressed misunderstandings, and given personal examples that have challenged me and offered practical solutions for everyday living. This book is a must-read for every believer, from the teacher to the student."

Lana Heightley, DPM
Women With A Mission
Colorado Springs, CO, USA

"Wendi Moen is a warrior-leader and encourager of the willing and a fearless lover of Jesus. She is at her best in demonstrating the fruit of the Spirit when she is taking on the unknown and bringing good news to the far reaches of the earth. She is one of the generation that stands in battle cry to encourage others in challenging times and declare that though we have seen the darkness, we are not afraid."

Jesse Adams, Ph.D.
VP of Business Development and Co-Founder, NanoLabz
Reno, NV, USA

"Wendi Moen skillfully reveals God's very nature to us in this wonderful book about the delicious and irresistible fruit of the Holy Spirit. Through her own transparent testimonies and biblical insight, she shows us how to cultivate and harvest His character within ourselves so that others truly see Jesus in us. Do you want to be more like God? Then this book is for you!"

Kathy Mooney
President, Reno/Sparks Aglow International.
Reno, NV, USA

Going After The Good Fruit will capture your heart! Wendi writes from a heart message that sows her life experience with solid biblical truth. She continues to encourage me with her character and faith. She is a forerunner of the present move of God. This book is a must-read to advance the Kingdom. I am privileged and honored to endorse this book.

Wendell McGowan
Senior Leader, Wendell McGowan Ministries
Las Vegas, NV, USA

What more can be said about the fruit of the Spirit? It's all been said already, right? Not so fast! In reading *Going After The Good Fruit*, Wendi shows the immediate importance of how necessary the fruit of the Spirit is in the lives of every believer in order to reveal the character of God in the earth so that others can know the revelation of Jesus for themselves. Pastor Wendi's insight is both funny and convicting. Get ready, because everything you thought you knew on this subject is about to change . . . and so is your life!

Jessica Nichols
Missions Pastor, Church Triumphant
Las Cruces, NM, USA

GOING AFTER THE GOOD FRUIT

God's Character: The Fruit of the Spirit

WENDI MOEN

Foreword by MARIO MURILLO

Dedication

I'd like to dedicate this book to my dear mother, who passed over to her eternal reward in August of 2011. Her life was a consistent reflection of the fruit of the Spirit in her journey on the earth. Her example of the fruit of the Spirit in her life was instrumental in setting me on my search to know the God who gives Himself freely to all who will ask.

Contents

Foreword

*T*he character of Christ does not appear in us by accident, automatically, or as a perk for being a Christian for a long time. It is both chilling and liberating when you discover that you have become stagnant in the fruit of the Holy Spirit.

It can be chilling to wake up one day and realize that you are no further along in your development as a loving and patient person than you were on the day you were born again. It can be liberating, as you will see when you read this book, if you choose to face your stagnation and grow. How truly wonderful it is, however, to know that you *can* come fully into His likeness and be filled with all of the riches of His character. You will discover then that God's greatest favor and provision fall to those who seek to be like Him.

In this book, Wendi is having the conversation that we don't want to have but we need to have. So much failure, cruelty, and hypocrisy are tolerated in the church because we secretly believe that purity of heart is a myth, an unachievable goal; as a result, we make allowances for political power plays, double standards, and glaring compromise.

Jesus said, "By this shall all men know that you are My disciples, if you have love for one another" (John 13:35). One of the greatest witnesses to the world is how Christians treat each other. One of the greatest excuses used against us is also how we treat each other.

The fruit of the Spirit are not a charming hobby to be sought by a few of us but a passionate pursuit to be revered by all of us. This book will instill a deep hunger in you to be like Jesus.

~Mario Murillo

Preface

One year I was invited to go on a mission trip to India and teach pastors and leaders on the fruit of the Spirit. Knowing the subject was important but not knowing a lot about it, at least not enough to teach on it, I decided to delve into the Scriptures further. The deeper my studies took me, the more intrigued I became on the nine character qualities of God and the requirement He sets forth as a command to display them on the earth.

Noticing that the difference between the *gifts* of the Spirit and the *fruit* of the Spirit and that both of these provisions from God in a believer's life are to be embraced, I decided to write this book as a tool for individual devotions or larger study groups. You will find the *Life Enhancement Journal* pages at the back of this book for those who desire to invest more time in study and in recording personal reflections and notes on the growth process.

This book is to train believers in how the fruit of the Spirit is produced and displayed in their lives. This fruit belongs to the Holy Spirit, who lives within us. The extent that we aggressively let Him produce and display this fruit in our lives separates us from those who say they know Him and yet lead lives that do not display the fruit of the Spirit from the Holy Spirit at work within them.

Acknowledgments

I want to give special thanks to my husband and best friend, Eric, for being a great example for me to follow. I watch your walk with God with a level of character and integrity that is to be commended and copied. Robbie, my son, I want to thank you for encouraging me and inspiring me to continue writing, even if it's only twenty words a day. My life has been changed for the better because of both of you.

I praise my Jesus for those of you that have taken time to read my chapters and give me honest feedback regarding its content, word usage, and the effects that it had on you as you reviewed them: Steve Backlund, Lana Heightley, Jim Wilson, Ila J. Henkel, and Linda Langley. Your feedback helped transform the outpour from my heart onto the pages in this book.

I'd also like to thank my amazing editor, Karen Roberts with RQuest, LLC, who continued to "remind me" of the need to finish this book. Without your gentle nudges, Karen, I'd still be waiting for some time tomorrow.

I also want to thank all those that have blessed me with opportunities to go aggressively after the fruit of the Spirit in ways that forced a growth in my character. Like I always say, everyone in your life is a blessing. God will bring people in your life to bless you because you can rest from your battles in knowing and spending time with them. He will bring others to you that cause you to reach deeper and higher on the tree of your life, where the fruit of the Spirit is waiting to be released, thus displaying the character and nature of God in greater ways.

God bless you as you venture out into the chapters of *Going After the Good Fruit* and let God transform you.

Chapter One

Move in the Gifts and Measure the Fruit

*H*ave you ever wondered how a tiny seed, when planted in the soil, given a little rain and sunshine from heaven, and then garnished with a kiss from God over a period of time, can blossom into a beautiful, robust, and productive tree? What is it about the apple tree that sets it apart from the orange tree or the lemon tree? Is it the apples themselves? Does an apple tree produce oranges? No, an apple tree produces apples. Does a lemon tree produce apples? No, a lemon tree produces only lemons, just as an orange tree produces only oranges. The tree portrays what it is by the fruit. Jesus expressed it best when He said:

"Either make the tree good and its fruit good, or make the tree bad and its fruit bad; for the tree is known by its fruit." ~Matthew 12:33

A Bushel and a Peck

How do you know if a tree is a healthy, "good" tree or a useless, "bad" tree? You know if a tree is good or bad by the fruit it produces—the amount of pecks or bushels of good fruit that you can measure after the harvest. Four pecks equal one bushel. The goal of the tree owner is to be able to measure a tree's fruit in bushels. In some cases, especially with young trees, pecks are a reasonable measurement to determine that the tree is an acceptable, fruit-bearing tree.

Not only does the volume of the fruit determine the health of a tree, but the fruit's size and flavor also determine if the tree is producing good or bad fruit. Healthy trees produce large, juicy fruit. Sickly trees produce fruit stunted in size and inferior taste. Many times I have purchased apples at the grocery store and taken them home with great anticipation of a tasty treat, only to bite into one and find it mushy. What about you? Or maybe you've eaten a dry orange. I don't think there's anything more disappointing to taste than bad fruit.

As it is with trees, so it is with Christians. The "produce" of their lives—in this book what I refer to as the fruit of the Spirit—must be able to be assessed in quantity and quality to determine if their lives are useful to God and worthy of His rewards.

"You will know them by their fruits. Grapes are not gathered from thorn bushes nor figs from thistles, are they? So every good tree bears good fruit, but the bad tree bears bad fruit. A good tree cannot produce bad fruit, nor can a bad tree produce good fruit. Every tree that does not bear good fruit is cut down and thrown into the fire. So then, you will know them by their fruits. Not everyone who says to Me, 'Lord, Lord,' will enter the kingdom of heaven, but he who does the will of My Father who is in heaven will enter. Many will say to Me on that day, 'Lord, Lord did we not prophesy in Your name, and in Your name cast out demons, and in Your name perform many miracles?'

And then I will declare to them, 'I never knew you; depart from Me, you who practice lawlessness.'" ~Matthew 7:16-23

This book is to train believers in how the fruit of the Spirit is produced and displayed in their lives. This fruit belongs to the Holy Spirit, who lives within us. The extent that we aggressively let Him produce and display this fruit in our lives separates us from those who say they know Him and yet lead lives that do not display the fruit of the Spirit from the Holy Spirit at work within them.

"But the fruit of the Spirit is love, joy, peace, patience, kindness, goodness, faithfulness, gentleness, self-control; against such things there is no law." ~Galatians 5:22-23

The original Greek word used for the word *fruit* in Galatians 5:22-23, as found in *Strong's Concordance*, is *karpos*. It means fruit as it is plucked, seized; to catch it away, to catch up, to pull and to take by force. It brings to the mind a picture of an aggressive and conscious effort to live in such a way that there is a consistent availability of the fruit of the Spirit in our lives. The fruit of the Spirit does not always appear without effort or just fall effortlessly from the tree of our lives to be used for God's purposes. Instead, it is a result of productivity, ready to be plucked and put to good use. Having the fruit of the Spirit requires purposeful acts to display it and apply it in our lives.

Having the fruit of the Spirit requires purposeful acts to display it and apply it in our lives.

Jesus spoke to the Pharisees, religious leaders of the day, saying that if they are claiming to live righteous and good lives, then the product of their lives will be able to be measured with good speech, which comes directly from the good treasure within their heart. That is, it would be through "good fruit" that "good trees" could be determined.

"Either make the tree good and its fruit good, or make the tree bad and its fruit bad; for the tree is known by its fruit. You brood of vipers, how can you, being evil, speak what is good? For the mouth speaks out of that which fills the heart. The good man brings out of his good treasure what is good; and the evil man brings out of his evil treasure what is evil." ~Matthew 12:33-35

Many people have mistaken the meaning of the "good fruit" spoken of by Jesus here in Matthew 12:33-35 to mean works and deeds done in life. The Greek word for *fruit* here is the same word used in Galatians 5:22-23, *karpos,* referring to the fruit of the Spirit. Later, as recorded in the New Testament, the apostle Paul does admonish that good works are very important; however, the Greek word he uses for *works* and the word Jesus uses for *fruit* are completely different words.

"For we are His workmanship, created in Christ Jesus for good works, which God prepared beforehand so that we would walk in them." ~Ephesians 2:10

The Greek word here for *works,* according to *Strong's Concordance,* is *ergon,* which means Paul admonishes us to "walk" in good *"works [ergon]"*; Jesus, in contrast, talks about having good *"fruit [karpos]."* Actually Paul combines the two thoughts in

Ephesians 2:10. He admonishes believers to "walk in," or perform, "good works" that display for use the fruit of the Spirit *goodness*— evidence of God's Spirit at work within us.

The Mission

Before we can fully realize the relationship the fruit has to the tree, we must understand the mission of the tree. Each tree has been given a purpose and a mission that stems from the intrinsic DNA of the seed. Every tree that bears good fruit has successfully drawn upon the power of the root system and has cultivated a beneficial relationship with the sun and the rain given to it by the mercy of God.

So it is with the relationship the Holy Spirit has to our lives. We must understand the mission that has been given to us. It is in our spiritual DNA, what we are to accomplish and become in this lifetime. When we give our lives to Jesus Christ, He gives us the Holy Spirit to help us become all that God has planned for us. We have the very DNA of heaven running through our blood. Lives that bear "good fruit"

> *We must understand the mission that has been given to us. It is in our spiritual DNA, what we are to accomplish and become in this lifetime.*

have successfully drawn upon the life-giving "root" force of God, the Holy Spirit, and have cultivated a loving and surrendered relationship to Him in order to display the very nature and character of God, which is the fruit of the Spirit.

The apostle Paul tells us that the Holy Spirit is given to us as a deposit and a guarantee. He is the deposit into our spirits, straight from heaven, that guarantees us eternal life and fulfillment of our mission on earth.

"Set his seal of ownership on us, and put his Spirit in our hearts as a deposit, guaranteeing what is to come." ~2 Corinthians 1:22 (NIV)

In his second letter to the Corinthian church, the apostle Paul reiterates this point.

"Now it is God who has made us for this very purpose and has given us the Spirit as a deposit, guaranteeing what is to come." ~2 Corinthians 5:5 (NIV)

Several places in Scripture tell us that God's good gifts to us, through the Holy Spirit within us, include the gifts, or manifestations, of the Holy Spirit. Here we see they are given in order to produce "for the common good."

"Now concerning spiritual gifts, brothers and sisters, I do not want you to be uninformed. You know that when you were pagans, you were enticed and led astray to idols that could not speak. Therefore I want you to understand that no one speaking by the Spirit of God ever says 'Let Jesus be cursed!' and no one can say 'Jesus is Lord' except by the Holy Spirit. Now there are varieties of gifts, but the same Spirit; and there are varieties of services, but the same Lord; and there are varieties of activities, but it is the same God who activates all of them in everyone. To each is given the manifestation of the Spirit for the common good. To one is given through the Spirit the utterance of wisdom, and to another the utterance of knowledge

according to the same Spirit, to another faith by the same Spirit, to another gifts of healing by the one Spirit, to another the working of miracles, to another prophecy, to another the discernment of spirits, to another various kinds of tongues, to another the interpretation of tongues. All these are activated by one and the same Spirit, who allots to each one individually just as the Spirit chooses." ~1 Corinthians 12:1-11 (NRSV)

The Holy Spirit fills us with both the *gifts* of the Spirit and the *fruit* of the Spirit. The gifts of the Spirit are released through us to empower us to restore the world back to God. The fruit of the Spirit is released through us as we are transformed more and more into His image. The power of the released gifts without the released fruit of the Spirit in our lives is profitless. Likewise, self-driven efforts to produce the fruit of the Spirit in our lives without the working of the power gifts of the Spirit are ineffective. Both the gifts of the Spirit and the fruit of the Spirit work together to manifest the fullness of God in our lives and in the lives of others.

In the Christian life, the life-giving source is the Holy Spirit. He releases the power of God, *gifts* of the Spirit as He wills, and also releases the character, personality, and nature of God, *karpos,* or *fruit* of the Spirit, as we call upon Him. The fruit of the Spirit, which is love, joy, peace, patience, kindness, goodness, faithfulness, gentleness, and self-control, is not produced through the workings of the gifts but rather through the Source of the gifts, which is the Holy Spirit. He is the ultimate giver and producer of both.

The gifts of the Spirit manifested through believers determine the effectiveness of power that the believers display in restoring unbelievers back to God; the fruit of the Spirit determines the destiny, health, and usefulness of the believers in reflecting God's image to the world. The fruit of the Spirit also determines the level of relationship, maturity, and rewards that the believers will have achieved when they stand face-to-face with God on the day of judgment.

Prophetic Picture of Gifts and Fruit Working Together

The Old Testament gives a prophetic picture of the gifts of the Spirit and the fruit of the Spirit working together. The prophetic picture appears as God is instructing the making of the priestly robe for ministry in the Temple.

"You shall make on its hem pomegranates of blue and purple and scarlet material, all around on its hem, and bells of gold between them all around: a golden bell and a pomegranate, a golden bell and a pomegranate, all around on the hem of the robe. It shall be on Aaron when he ministers; and its tinkling shall be heard when he enters and leaves the holy place before the LORD, so that he will not die." ~Exodus 28:33-35

In the placement of the pomegranates between each bell all around the hem of the priest's robe, we can see a prophetic picture of the fruit of the Spirit and the gifts of the Spirit working together to accomplish God's purposes. The pomegranates represent the fruit of the Spirit; the bells represent the gifts of the Spirit. The bells created a "tinkling" sound that could be heard when the priest entered and left the Holy Place while ministering before the Lord. The pomegranates, spaced between the bells, prevented the bells from beating together loudly as the priest walked, which would have created a harsh, clanging noise. God wanted the "tinkle."

The bells served their purpose by releasing the tinkling sound that there was movement and action as the priest walked around the Temple. So it is with the gifts of the Spirit. They make a sound to the world as they are released so that those who have ears to hear and conviction to respond will be reunited with God, who loves them. The pomegranates allowed the sound of the bells to be pleasing to God's ears and those receiving the ministry of the priest. Here is an example of the fruit and the gifts working together. The fruit of the Spirit *love* is a "buffering" agent for the gifts of the Spirit to work in full force without sounding like a "noisy, clanging cymbal" to God and those receiving the ministry of God.

Gifts of the Spirit Empower Us

Our mission is given to us by Jesus Christ, through the Holy Spirit, to glorify God's authority and display His power through the gifts of the Spirit. This display of heavenly power is to assure all of mankind that God is the King of all the earth. God expects us to move in that power and

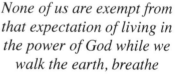

None of us are exempt from that expectation of living in the power of God while we walk the earth, breathe His air, drink His water, and eat His food.

authority, through the name of His Son Jesus, the All-Powerful One. None of us are exempt from that expectation of living in the power of God while we walk the earth, breathe His air, drink His water, and eat His food. We have been saved and empowered to carry on the mission of Jesus when He left the earth and ascended into heaven.

"Little children, make sure no one deceives you; the one who practices righteousness is righteous, just as He is righteous; the one who practices sin is of the devil; for the devil has sinned from the beginning. The Son of God appeared for this purpose, to destroy the works of the devil." ~1 John 3:7-9

The mission we have been given from Jesus is to destroy the works of the devil by displaying the power of God through the *gifts* of the Spirit. Look again at these specific verses in 2 Corinthians chapter 12.

"Now there are varieties of gifts, but the same Spirit. And there are varieties of ministries, and the same Lord. There are varieties of effects, but the same God who works all things in all persons. But to each one is given the manifestation of the Spirit for the common good. For to one is given the word of wisdom through the Spirit, and to another the word of knowledge according to the same Spirit; to another faith by the same Spirit, and to another gifts of healing by the one Spirit, and to another the effecting of miracles, and to another prophecy, and to another the distinguishing of spirits, to another various kinds of tongues, and to another the interpretation of tongues. But one and the same Spirit works all these things, distributing to each one individually just as He wills." ~Corinthians 12:4-11

Each of the gifts the Holy Spirit manifested through believers allows nonbelievers to know that God is real. When the gifts *wisdom* and *knowledge* are manifested toward nonbelievers, in a form only they and God know, then they see that God knows all secrets and mysteries along with the thoughts and intentions of their hearts. The scriptural purposes for this revelation are to convince them of God's sovereign knowledge of and intimacy toward them and to lead them to repentance.

When the gifts *faith, healing,* and *prophesy* are manifested through believers, then nonbelievers see that the supernatural has invaded the natural with the purpose to bring glory to God. When the gifts *distinguishing of spirits, tongues, interpretation,* and *effecting of miracles* are manifested, revelation is released, and God's voice is heard through the ungodly noise of the world. Humanity is once again drawn back and given the opportunity to be restored in relationship to the Creator.

Fruit of the Spirit Measures the Success

Just as manifestations of the power of God through the gifts of the Spirit are a measure of the success in our Christian walk, so also are the displays of the fruit of the Spirit in our lives. God requires us to be successful in living out the character, personality, and nature of God,

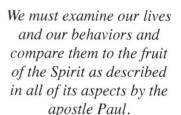

We must examine our lives and our behaviors and compare them to the fruit of the Spirit as described in all of its aspects by the apostle Paul.

which is the *fruit* of the Spirit. God measures the harvest of this fruit, the quantity and quality of fruit of the Spirit in our daily lives. So that He can do so and see an abundance, we must examine our lives and our behaviors and compare them to the fruit of the Spirit as described in all of its aspects by the apostle Paul.

"But the fruit of the Spirit is love, joy, peace, patience, kindness, goodness, faithfulness, gentleness, self-control; against such things there is no law." ~Galatians 5:22-23

How much do we love? How often do we experience joy? What is the level of peace? Is our patience evident to those around us? Do we act with kindness and goodness even when we feel the situations do not deserve it? Are we faithful in the midst of adversity? Do we react with gentleness and self-control when harshness and injustice are screaming around us? This fruit is easy to see and measurable as it is manifested in our lives. When it is consistently evident, we succeed in pleasing God as we fulfill our heavenly mission for Him here on earth.

Since our mission is to continue the work of Jesus, to destroy the works of the devil as we interact with people who are bound by him (1 John 3:9), we inevitably encounter situations that come up against us and challenge our behavior. By learning how to live in the power of the Spirit so that we display the fruit of the Spirit on a daily basis, we overcome the influence the devil can have on our own emotions and reactions toward others. We find ourselves having greater success over the oppression and influence the devil can have in our own circumstances as we continually and consistently move forward, destroying his influence in other people's lives.

Without the fruit of the Spirit being on display as we perform the mission given to us by God, it's quite clear from Scripture that our exploits in His name will not bring profit in the end. Note the emphasis on the fruit in the passage that follows. In this case, the specific fruit is *love*—love for Him and love for others.

"If I speak with the tongues of men and of angels, but do not have love, I have become a noisy gong or a clanging cymbal. I have the gift of prophecy, and know all mysteries and all knowledge; and if I have all faith, so as to remove mountains, but do not have love, I am nothing. And if I give all my possessions to feed the poor, and if I surrender my body to be burned, but do not have love, it profits me nothing." ~1 Corinthians 13:1-3

As you move forward in this book, you will see more about the fruit of the Spirit *love* and all other fruit of the Spirit in fuller context.

Fruit of the Spirit Measures the Reward

The gifts of the Spirit *tongues, prophecy, discernment* (of spirits, knowing which spiritual force is at work in the situation at hand), and *faith* (which includes giving, sacrifice, martyrdom, and believing God for the impossible) are useful to us in determining how to minister to those receiving our service. When we get to heaven and stand before God, however, it will be the *fruit* of the Spirit having been displayed in our lives that will get God's attention and move His hand to reward us. God desires to bless us for our obedience to Him. The favorable profit and reward in heaven is being laid up there for us when our good works are performed and completed along with the display of the fruit of His Spirit. He rewards us according to the fruit of the Spirit that accompanies our actions.

"And if I give all my possessions to feed the poor, and if I surrender my body to be burned, but do not have love, it profits me nothing." ~1 Corinthians 13:3

Giving your possessions to the poor is a wonderful act of obedience and for many a great sacrifice requiring great measures of faith. In Matthew's account of Jesus interacting with the rich, young ruler regarding the subject of getting into heaven, Jesus told him to keep the commandments and then verbalized a few of the Ten Commandments. This comment didn't seem to satisfy the young man, so he responded back to Jesus as if there must be more to bring fulfillment to his life.

"The young man said to Him, 'All these things I have kept; what am I still lacking?' Jesus said to him, 'If you wish to be complete, go and sell your possessions and give to the poor, and you will have treasure in heaven; and come, follow Me.'" ~Matthew 19:20-22

According to this passage, giving to the poor would "complete" the young man. The last part of Jesus' answer to him is one not to overlook. We read it, but often we fail to accomplish it: "Come, follow Me."

Surrendering your body to be burned would also be considered a valiant sacrifice for the Kingdom of God, as Jesus mentioned when conversing to His disciples regarding being His friend.

"And if I give all my possessions to feed the poor, and if I surrender my body to be burned, but do not have love, it profits me nothing." ~1 Corinthians 13:3

We can see in these passages of Scripture that giving to the poor and laying your life down by surrendering your body for your friend are both amazing acts of sacrifice and obedience. There remains, however, still a greater truth set forth by Jesus. This truth is to display the fruit of the Spirit *love* toward one another.

"This is My commandment, that you love one another, just as I have loved you. Greater love has no one than this, that one lay down his life for his friends. You are My friends if you do what I command you." ~John 15:12-14

Notice how He ends His statement, summarizing exactly what is required to be His friend.

"You are My friends if you do what I command you." ~John 15:14

Fulfilling the command to love is what it takes to be Jesus' friend.

Fulfilling the command to love is what it takes to be Jesus' friend.

The Display of the Fruit of the Spirit *Love*

Love, the first in the list of the fruit of the Spirit in Galatians 5, defines the measure of our friendship with Jesus. As we move in His power, through the gifts of the Spirit, there is a requirement by Jesus that love is present. The display of the fruit of the Spirit *love*, as we employ the gifts of the Spirit He has given us to use, determines the profit and the reward.

"But love your enemies, and do good, and lend, expecting nothing in return; and your reward will be great, and you will be sons of

the Most High; for He Himself is kind to ungrateful and evil men."
~Luke 6:35

Notice too in this passage that when measuring the fruit of the Spirit in our lives, Jesus even goes a step further and requires three specific fruit—*love, goodness,* and *kindness*—to be manifested upon those that don't deserve it. Yes, even our enemies, which implies especially our enemies. And then He asks a rhetorical question regarding this requirement.

"If you love those who love you, what reward do you have? Do not even the tax collectors do the same?" ~Matthew 5:46

If I were accustomed to living my life with a false religious humility, I might say, "It doesn't matter if I get rewarded from God. I don't do things for the rewards anyway." As noble as this statement may sound, it is flawed. God desires to reward me. If I act in ways that rob God's provision to reward me (acting on my own, outside of His power), I am robbing God of opportunities to express His nature toward me. *He* desires to lavish His love, goodness, and kindness on *me*.

God is good all the time, and it's the kindness of God that leads to repentance. He has given me a responsibility to display His goodness and His kindness toward those around me, including those that don't deserve it. He desires to release goodness and kindness on me and upon the people of the earth through me. Luke says it best.

"For He Himself is kind to ungrateful and evil men." ~Luke 6:35

In many cases, the opposite is true of us. When we are wronged, we are conditioned by the world to bring judgment upon those that wronged us. We are quick to set ourselves up as judges, trying to read into the hearts of others and determine their motives for their actions, especially when it comes to spiritual issues.

In 2004, as I was on a mission trip to the Philippines, this truth was evident in my life. After each powerful night of music, drama, testimonies, and preaching, our leadership team gave an altar call and challenged the people to give their lives to Jesus. Night after night we preached to thousands of people, and every night hundreds of people would respond to the call of God upon their lives. On the third night with these victorious altar calls of hundreds at a time coming forward to give their hearts to Jesus, I began to think, "Oh, they are just coming forward because we're Americans. They don't really mean it."

Not even two seconds went by after I had the thought when God, through the Holy Spirit, reprimanded me very firmly. He said, "I called you to preach the gospel, not judge the heart of man." He said it in such a way that it sent a holy fear through my soul. He was not pleased with me or the thought I had entertained while judging the motives of those converts. The apostle Paul put in words how I should have responded.

"Therefore do not go on passing judgment before the time, but wait until the Lord comes who will both bring to light the things hidden in the darkness and disclose the motives of men's hearts; and then each man's praise will come to him from God." ~1 Corinthians 4:5

The fruit of the Spirit begins inside of us as a motive of the heart. God judges the works that I do, and the reward is given to me according to what motivates me to perform these works. Do I speak in tongues, prophesy, or give my body to be burned because I love? The point is this: Rewards are given to each man, woman, and child on the judgment day in heaven according to the motives of the heart, which are the foundation under each action.

The fruit of the Spirit begins inside of us as a motive of the heart.

Since motives of the heart are not always perfected as quickly as our ability to obey the truth, God makes provision by telling us it's better to obey than to sacrifice (1 Samuel 15:22). There have been times that God has required me to obey Him in the Christian disciplines of tithing, praying, reading the Scriptures, and attending church and Bible studies. My heart was not always cheerful at the time, but as I obeyed the Scriptures in these areas, my heart was changed for the better. Obeying the word of God allows God to perfect the motives of the heart and ultimately allow the fruit of the Spirit to be perfected in our lives.

Obeying the word of God allows God to perfect the motives of the heart and ultimately allow the fruit of the Spirit to be perfected in our lives.

I love to travel to the nations and preach the gospel. I am continually tested, however, on why I go. Do I travel to the nations because I just want to get away from my current situations? Or do I go to the nations because of the fruit of the Spirit *love* for the souls and their spiritual need for Jesus? If I go out of simple obedience and call upon the Holy Spirit to display the love that is required to bring forth the harvest, it will be counted and profited to my "account" in heaven. So before I go, many times I pray like this: "Jesus, you said that the one who is forgiven much, loves much. Show me where I need forgiveness so I can have more love in my heart for the lost." Another great, heartfelt prayer that God loves to hear from me is this one: "Lord, increase the capacity of my heart to love." He is faithful always to show me my need for forgiveness and to release more of His love in my heart.

Seeing our own sin and need for forgiveness is a great beginning in releasing more of His love for others in our hearts. The release of that love is what He rewards.

Fruit of the Spirit Measures the Relationship

As a child of God, I must focus on developing a love relationship with Him first, knowing that all the power He has will flow through me naturally as I surrender to who He is. He expects me to display His love laced in His power. Joy, peace, patience, goodness, kindness, faithfulness, gentleness, and self-control, the other fruit of the Spirit, are also character qualities and behaviors that become more and more evident as His power is released in and through my life—that is, if I want what I do for Him to be credited to my account in heaven.

A good example of this truth, that my relationship with Him comes first, is portrayed in my relationship with my own son. When my son was entering into his adolescence, he only had one consistent chore required of him to contribute to the operation of our household. He was responsible for taking the trash out to the street for pickup. This chore involved emptying the trash buckets in every room into a large trash bag and then transferring that bag to the large garage can.

He was then to haul that can out to the street, where the community garbage service would empty it into a truck the next morning. The whole process for my son was about a ten-minute job that required simple effort and timing. If he missed the community pickup, then we were stuck with the garbage for another week or we had to pay to take it to the dump. On the eve of trash day, the scenario between my son and me would look and sound something like this.

"Son, don't forget to take the garbage out to the curb tonight before you go to bed. Tomorrow's trash day comes early, and I know you'll be tired in the morning before school."

Coming from his bedroom, in his most obedient and loving voice, my son's reply would be, "Okay, Mom. I'll do it in a minute."

While I continued washing the dinner dishes, my attention hung on his words of brief postponement. After twenty minutes, I would realize selfishly that my great amount of patience was being ignored. I had expected to see him come down at any moment and begin gathering the garbage as I had lovingly requested almost a half hour earlier. So once again I would call up to him "Son, are you going to take the garbage out like I asked you?"

Promptly he would yell down in a not-such-a-loving voice this time, "I said that I'll be down in a minute."

I would then wait for about thirty more intense, silent minutes. Finally, from deep within the walls of my belly, I would feel my firmest mommy voice rise to the surface with the intensity that I knew would get instant results. I would then deliver my final command with all parental authority that only a mother can give. "Son, I asked you to do something for me an hour ago. I need you to stop what you are doing and get going on it right now. I don't mean in

40

another hour from now or when you get around to it. Now, get down here, please, and take the trash out. NOW!"

Within seconds I would hear the bedroom door open. With every step of his coming closer, I could hear the huffing and puffing of a very perturbed thirteen-year-old who was mumbling under his breath while stomping down the stairs. He'd push his way past me without an acknowledgment of my existence, sling open the cupboard under the sink, and grab the kitchen trash dispenser. After slamming the cupboard door, he'd go from room to room, throwing the emptied trash buckets down as he combined the trash into the one community bag. With obvious anger, he'd jerk his lanky 5'2" adolescent body around like a charging elephant in a china shop. At last out the door he'd bolt, dragging the large, green garbage can to the curb.

Now remember, he'd been given only one assignment a week, to take out the garbage. Did he end up taking out the garbage? Yes. Was I thrilled when the task was completed? No. Why? Because what was done in obedience was not motivated by love for me. The level of love and honor displayed during the performing of his task was far below what our relationship deserved after its thirteen years of cultivation.

Was taking the trash out a good thing? Yes. Did the entire family benefit for having the trash taken out? Yes. Was doing it a benefit to our relationship? No. In fact, the results were just the opposite. Why? My son's completion of the task was not motivated by his relationship of love for me; instead, it was motivated by his obligation to perform because it was his job.

Did my son get any credit with me or receive any special favor while he was performing his task? No. In fact, he got no points with me whatsoever. It was all I could do not to inflict severe discipline on him for his lack of respect and honor. The way my son performed the task was like a disgruntled servant or afflicted slave might, not like a loving son would for his beloved mother. Because I expected more from our relationship, no reward was given for his grudging obedience. Instead, he robbed me of my joy and desire to bless him for his obedience.

Doing God's "Chores" with Love

Do you see the parallel? God feels in a similar way about us. If we perform our tasks with the mind of Christ, displaying the fruit of the Spirit as we move in the power of the gifts, our rewards are great. As a result, God's true identity is made known to the world in greater measure. See the words of apostle Paul that admonish on this point.

"Therefore if there is any encouragement in Christ, if there is any consolation of love, if there is any fellowship of the Spirit, if any affection and compassion, make my joy complete by being of the same mind, maintaining the same love, united in spirit, intent on one purpose. Do nothing from selfishness or empty conceit, but with humility of mind regard one another as more important than yourselves; do not merely look out for your own personal interests, but also for the interests of others. Have this attitude in yourselves which was also in Christ Jesus, who, although He existed in the form of God, did not regard equality with God a thing to be grasped, but emptied Himself, taking the form of a bond-servant, and being made in the likeness of men. Being found in appearance as a man, He humbled Himself by becoming obedient to the point of death, even death on a cross. For this reason also, God highly exalted Him, and bestowed on Him

the name which is above every name, so that at the name of Jesus EVERY KNEE WILL BOW, of those who are in heaven and on earth and under the earth, and that every tongue will confess that Jesus Christ is Lord, to the glory of God the Father." ~Philippians 2:1-11 (emphasis mine)

As parents and stewards of the children God has given us, we are to teach our children the importance of the fruit of the Spirit in their lives as well. I continued to parent my son, encouraging him to grow in love and obedience and self-control. He has grown into a wonderful, godly man now living on his own, graduated from college in Southern California with a communications degree and influential with his faith in the broadcasting and film industry. He has told me he runs into opportunities every day to release the fruit of the Spirit in his life.

Displaying the fruit is a part of our lifelong journey with God. We learn how to do it, in part, through obedient submission.

Displaying the fruit is a part of our lifelong journey with God. We learn how to do it, in part, through obedient submission. As we are intentional about submitting to the Holy Spirit for its release, the fruit of the Spirit becomes more evident in our lives.

Fruit of the Spirit Measures the Maturity

The display of the fruit of the Spirit allows the Spirit to measure how we are progressing in our growth and maturity in the reflection of God's image through us on the earth. The Holy Spirit resides in our bodies to give us the power to choose to live a life in full surrender to God and all that He has for us. His character, personality, nature, and power that flow through us as fruit define the maturity of our relationship in Him. The character, personality, and nature of God are manifested through the *fruit* of the Spirit; the power of God is manifested through the *gifts* of the Spirit; and the fullness of God is manifested through the combination of the *fruit* and the *gifts* working together at full throttle!

Spiritual Maturity in the Fruit and Gifts of the Spirit

God didn't design us to live out our lives only by gifts or only by fruit. Our life in Christ was not intended to be an either/or proposition (fruit or gifts) or a you-choose-what-fits-your-personality-best endeavor. The gifts and the fruit are both necessary to reach full maturity. One without the other just does not lead us into a mature spiritual life in Christ.

The gifts and the fruit are both necessary to reach full maturity. One without the other just does not lead us into a mature spiritual life in Christ.

Focusing on the gifts of the Spirit without equal focus on the display of good fruit of the Spirit makes some believers haughty. It also gives immature believers a false sense of assurance that they have something others do not. Thinking that you have obtained extra favor with God and position in heaven for great exploits performed on the earth through the gifts leads only to false illusions on earth and disappointment on judgment day. If you are majoring in one and neglecting the other, then you are like a one-legged person trying to peddle a bicycle uphill in a mudslide. In other words, honoring one above the other will only lead to imbalance, weakness, and ineffective labor. Remember, power without love is just as noisy as clanging cymbals to God's ears (1 Corinthians 13:1).

In the same way, placing a higher honor on the fruit of the Spirit in your life over the gifts can lead you to justify the lack of using the gifts God has given you for His purposes—also not a sign of spiritual maturity. By placing an overemphasis on the fruit without the gifts, you can come to believe that you can win others to the Lord by just being a really nice person. This focus can cause you to disdain those that move in the gifts of the Spirit. Some believers who do not embrace the power of the gifts go so far as to mock with contempt and judge with jealousy those they see using the gifts, especially the gifts of tongues or prophecy. By moving into judgment and jealousy, they nullify the very fruit of the Spirit they have to offer the world.

So you can see how gifts without the fruit or fruit without the gifts can launch you into a vicious spiritual tailspin. It can cause you to revert to what you know best, and that is the behavior of the flesh, which inevitably ends in destruction and death. (Chapter 3 addresses this issue in more depth.)

Thankfully, Jesus is our example and guide. He expects us to walk in the *fullness* of His Spirit, which is accomplished by moving and functioning in the *gifts* while displaying our maturity through the *fruit* of the Spirit in our lives. In the apostle Paul's letter to the Ephesians, he urges believers to reach for the fullness of the Spirit in their lives.

"For this reason I bow my knees before the Father, from whom every family in heaven and on earth derives its name, that He would grant you, according to the riches of His glory, to be strengthened with power through His Spirit in the inner man, so that Christ may dwell

in your hearts through faith; and that you, being rooted and grounded in love, may be able to comprehend with all the saints what is the breadth and length and height and depth, and to know the love of Christ which surpasses knowledge, that you may be filled up to all the fullness of God." ~Ephesians 3:14-19

In this passage, Paul exhorts believers to be filled up to all the fullness of God by being strengthened with power through the gift of the Spirit *faith,* all the while being rooted and grounded in the fruit of the Spirit *love.* By having the working of both the gift and the fruit in full operation in their lives, believers can know the *love* (fruit) of Christ, which surpasses *knowledge* (gift), and be filled with the fullness of God.

Time to Pray

If God has spoken to you during this chapter and you desire to release more of the gifts and display more of the fruit of the Spirit in your life, then pray with me right now.

"God, I come to You right now in Jesus name, and I ask You for Your forgiveness. My desire is to be filled to full capacity with the Holy Spirit. I ask You to release all the gifts of the Spirit in me as mentioned in 1 Corinthians 12:4-11. I also pray that You begin to give me discernment when the fruit of the Spirit is not being displayed in my life. I want to walk in the fruit of the Spirit through prayer and proclamation and release freedom in my life to live in the fullness of God. In Jesus' name, amen."

Time to Apply

After you have spent time with the Holy Spirit and finished recording your answers in your *Life Enhancement Journal* at the back of the book, proceed to Chapter Two: *Consider the Fruit Tree.*

Chapter Two

Consider the Fruit Tree

When I was ten years old, I lived in a small town in the desert of Southern California called Cherry Valley. I loved Cherry Valley because it was always dry and extremely warm. My family's modest ranch-style home sat on five acres, which included two pastures, a small barn, and a cherry orchard. I lived with my mom, dad, and two younger sisters. I had a great passion for animals, and my parents made sure we had plenty of them.

I had two appaloosa horses named Cala and China Doll, a Shetland pony called Mr. Bitts, a calf affectionately labeled Little Lu-Lu, a Siamese cat nicknamed Tu-Tu, and a German shepherd dog, Belle, who was the queen of the pack. Occasionally I'd adopt a pet garter snake I'd find in the canyons adjacent to our home. I never shared my devotion with it long enough to name it. I just liked knowing that I could periodically conquer the wild. I wasn't particularly fond of spiders either, but every now and then I'd find a big, hairy tarantula nestled in the hay at feeding time and capture it with an empty peanut butter jar, poking holes in the top of the lid to sustain its life while it suffered in such a confined space.

We didn't have a fenced arena for exercising my show horse, China Doll, so I would ride her in our cherry orchard in front of the house. I discovered that if I rode China Doll around the perimeter of the orchard, I could eventually create a worn down path that was level enough to use as my own fenceless arena. China Doll was amazingly smart and would graciously humor my efforts to keep her on the homemade path.

One hot July afternoon as I was exercising China Doll in the orchard, I became very hungry. I deviated from the routine of the path and trotted her up to one of the ripening cherry trees. My plan was to grab some cherries off the tree for a snack, but when I got up to the tree, I noticed that all the cherries within my reach had already fallen to the ground and had started to rot or had been picked by the birds. I decided I would turn China Doll into an equine ladder and climb the tree to reach the fruit I needed at that moment to satisfy my desire for summer snacking.

Very carefully I nudged her up to the tree, held on to the reins while steadying my feet on her back, and began slowly climbing up to reach the branches that had fruit available for eating. To my frustration, many cherries were higher than I could reach. I knew at that point if I wanted to collect more fruit, I would have to take China Doll back to the house and return with a real ladder to make my way up to the top of the tree for a greater harvest.

After reflecting on this childhood memory of aggressively going after the cherries that were out of my reach to satisfy my hunger, I started

> *Some fruit of the Spirit is harder to display and walk in than other fruit. Other fruit of the Spirit can seem far out of reach, especially in times of testing and distress.*

understanding more about the need to use this same aggressive approach toward the fruit of the Spirit in my life. Some fruit of the Spirit is harder to display and walk in than other fruit. Other fruit of the Spirit can seem far out of reach, especially in times of testing and distress.

Still after All These Years

I received Jesus Christ into my life in 1978 through a revelation of God's unconditional love and a vision of Jesus Christ on the cross. I was looking for love that would not fail me. I knew my friends and even my earthly family were able to love me with a love that would only satisfy the surface of my very deep soul's hunger. In my desperate need to fill the dark chasm of emptiness, I cried out to God in my bedroom one night. I wanted to experience the unconditional love that had always pointed to Him.

"God is love, God is love," kept looping in my mind like a broken record. I fell to my knees and prayed, "God, if You are love, I want You, I need You in my life." At that moment, I saw a vision of Jesus on the cross and said, "Jesus, I really don't know what You have to do with anything, but if You come with God, then I want You too. I want all of You. I want everything God has for me because I know that God is love, and I need love." The vision dissipated, and I fell asleep on the floor.

After a few hours, I awoke. It was around 2 a.m., but I had the most insatiable urge to find a Bible and begin reading it. I found one on a dusty bookshelf in the living room, turned to the first New Testament book, Matthew, and began reading about the life of Jesus Christ. I was amazed at His life and power as I read about the miracles and the compassion He had for all humanity. I began to speak with Jesus about those things I was reading. For example, when I read that He healed the sick and raised the dead, I said to Him with amazement, "Wow, Jesus. I had no idea You did those things."

After communing with Jesus for about an hour, He then spoke to me very clearly. "Wendi, now that you know Me, let Me introduce you to My Father."

Within a moment, the heavens opened. Jesus unveiled my spiritual eyes and introduced me to God the Father. The presence of God seemed to swallow me up and overtake all my passions. I was filled with inexpressible amazement that I was meeting Jesus' Father, Almighty God, Creator of me and the universe. I instinctively knew Jesus' Father was my Father also, and this truth completely and literally floored me. I fell face down on the floor in worship to His revealed majesty, fearing that if I looked up and gazed into the heavens again, I would melt into a puddle of liquid flesh.

When the weighty presence of God lifted after about thirty minutes, I tentatively got up, one vertebrae at a time, out of my prostrate position. Again I was visited with an open-eyed vision. This time I witnessed a man, dressed in white, with long hair, sitting on a white horse with massive wings that were exiting out my bedroom window. I knew this man had to be Jesus. I gazed in wonder as He flew out of my window, into the early morning air, straight into heaven.

My life was changed radically at that moment, and I have never been the same. My heart was so deeply transformed. All I wanted to do was to know Jesus Christ and do things that pleased my Father God. I no longer desired to think like the world or be a part of the evil desires of my former lust for self-satisfaction.

Baptised in the Holy Spirit

One year after I was transferred into the Kingdom of light through my faith in Jesus Christ, the fiery presence of God visited me again. This time I was in my car, driving home from a singles' Bible study in Chico, California. The Holy Spirit baptised me with the consuming fire of His power, evidenced in the days and years to come by many spiritual gifts.

"Now there are varieties of gifts, but the same Spirit. And there are varieties of ministries, and the same Lord. There are varieties of effects, but the same God who works all things in all persons. But to each one is given the manifestation of the Spirit for the common good. For to one is given the word of wisdom through the Spirit, and to another the word of knowledge according to the same Spirit; to another faith by the same Spirit, and to another gifts of healing by the one Spirit, and to another the effecting of miracles, and to another prophecy, and to another the distinguishing of spirits, to another various kinds of tongues, and to another the interpretation of tongues."
~1 Corinthians 12:4-10

How can it be that after thirty years of dedicated service to God, I still can slip into less-than-godly actions, completely based on how someone else treats me with conditional love? After all I know about heaven and the ways of God, how is it that I can still make decisions in my life that benefit my agendas above those of others? And why do I still sometimes perform tasks based on convenience to my ways and my world and lose hold of my ability to be in control of my own behaviors? If the fruit of the Spirit is love, joy, peace, patience, goodness, kindness, faithfulness, gentleness, and self-control, why do I still experience periodic depression and anxiety, emotional chaos, and a mean spirit that speaks harsh words when I'm hurt or upset? How can I act in ways that are not glorifying to the holiness of God?

Because I am a mature believer, it seems as if it should be easier for me to reflect the Kingdom of light now more than ever before. Wouldn't you think, after almost three decades of walking hand in hand with Jesus, seeing visions, encountering angels, casting out demons, and healing the sick, that my behavior would be almost impeccable in exemplifying the fruit of the Spirit?

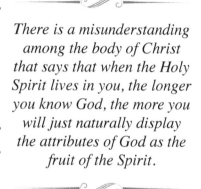

There is a misunderstanding among the body of Christ that says that when the Holy Spirit lives in you, the longer you know God, the more you will just naturally display the attributes of God as the fruit of the Spirit.

There is a misunderstanding among the body of Christ that says that when the Holy Spirit lives in you, the longer you know God, the

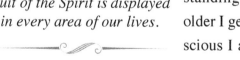

Aggressive action is needed on our part to insure that the fruit of the Spirit is displayed in every area of our lives.

more you will just naturally display the attributes of God as the fruit of the Spirit. I find this misunderstanding to be troublesome. The older I get in the Lord, the more conscious I am of where I fall short in fulfilling God's best in my life. The truth is, aggressive action is needed on our part to insure that the fruit of the Spirit is displayed in every area of our lives.

Sing 'Em Again!

Songs have been written by myriads of artists that talk about the need for the fruit of the Spirit *love,* though it is not labeled as such. Hal David and Burt Bacharach's hit song called "What the World Needs Now" declares that the world needs love, "not just for some, but for everyone." Black Eyed Peas has taken the song "Where Is the Love?" and made a video for their fans. Could this song's message truly be the cry of these musicians' hearts? Better question: Can the love the world is searching for come from me? After all, I know God, God lives in me, and God is love.

Hoyt Axton wrote a whimsical song called "Jeremiah Was a Bullfrog" in which he proclaims, "Joy to the world, all the boys and girls. Joy to the fishes in the deep blue sea. Joy to you and me." He is wishing joy to come upon the whole world, including the fish in the sea. He begs for the *joy* fruit of the Spirit to be evident in the world; I have it living within me. Am I living out my life, allowing the Holy Spirit to display His joy everyday to all those around me?

What about walking in the fruit of the Spirit *peace* in every circumstance? "Let There Be Peace On Earth," written by Jill Jackson Miller and Sy Miller, is a plea for brothers and sisters to avail themselves to the peace (of God, implied); and "let it begin with me" is their prayer. This peace, like the love and joy in these other songs, is available to us through the fruit of the Spirit. I've recognized that in my life, when the winds of adversity are blowing, when the boat of my reactions is rocking, when the trees of my expectations are uprooted, and when the chaos of circumstances comes knocking at my door, much of the time my peace is tempted to fly right out the window like a frantic, trapped bird that just encountered the way of escape. My ability to be peaceful in the chaos is the result of a conscious effort on my part to discern its absence and then call upon the Holy Spirit to be peace *in* me. "Peace of heaven, come" is a prayer that I live by.

Patience? Ha! Guns N' Roses sings out, "Just a little patience is all we need." I think this group is on to something. What the singers don't know is that patience has been given through the fruit of the Spirit. If knowing this is true, then why is it, when the going gets tough, this spiritual giant of a woman is tempted to let the "fur fly" off the fan of her existence and nail the closest human to the wall? Not all the time, but enough times that it convicts me of the need to "pageant" more patience in my life. I know that the fruit of the Spirit is available to flow in greater measures through me in this area if I'd aggressively go after the Holy Spirit to produce it and display it.

> *I know that the fruit of the Spirit is available to flow in greater measures through me in this area if I'd aggressively go after the Holy Spirit to produce it and display it.*

David Wilcox, in a song called "Kindness," lists all the great things he loves in a person. The hook of the song fastens it all together in the line, "but it's your kindness that shines so bright." The kindness this woman shows is the greatest feature that draws him in to loving her. Likewise, the fruit of the Spirit *kindness* unmistakably affects mankind when it beautifully clothes a human life. As a child of the Most Kind King, where is that kindness that I can lavish upon a disgruntled coworker, overbearing boss, imperfect husband, or rebellious two-year-old who has a two-word vocabulary of "no" and "gimme"?

I also have put music to some of the fruit of the Spirit. In "Psalm 23" on my album *Loving You,* the line, "surely goodness and mercy shall follow me all the days of my life" precedes the phrase "and I shall dwell in the house of the Lord forever and ever." The *goodness* fruit of the Spirit must have been significant to King David to cause him to combine it with the word *mercy* when he wrote that psalm's final phrase. He could have said "love and mercy" or "patience and mercy" or any other of the fruit of the Spirit plus mercy. But He didn't. He specifically wrote "goodness and mercy."

If the *goodness* fruit of the Spirit is in me and is displayed through the Holy Spirit, then why does it seem to go intermittently dormant when I'm expected to perform tasks that don't fit my personality, gifts, or energy level? It's always easier to let someone else perform acts of goodness. Do you know the old saying, "If you want something done, have someone else do it, but if you want something done right, do it yourself, of course, with an attitude"? I do, and I think you know what I'm talking about!

Raphael Saadiq's song called "Faithful" says, "I'm faithful to my baby, to cheat on you would be crazy. I can't cheat on you, I can't do it no more." Wow. He and those he sings to know and accept that cheating is wrong. Here is a man who confesses he is faithful and won't cheat on his lover. Of the many faces and expressions of faithfulness, fidelity in relationship is just one. What about faithfulness to committed tasks, to promises, and so on? I may be able to be faithful in my relationships, but what about things I've committed to do for others? Does my faithfulness only reach so far until I get bored or feel used, abused, unappreciated, or taken advantage of?

Why is it so easy to forget about "going the extra mile" that Jesus talks about?

"Whoever forces you to go one mile, go with him two." ~Matthew 5:41

Is it because completing the original "mile" is challenging enough? If the weather is perfect, my hair looks just right, I'm not mad at anyone, or I haven't gotten any dirty looks from anyone else, then maybe, just maybe, I'll do what I said I'd do or complete a task that I started. Oh, and you want a smile with that menial act of obedience too!

I do not want to forget to display the easygoing, soft-spoken *gentleness* fruit of the Spirit. What's that? Harsh words, cold shoulder, snippy attitudes—at times I'd rather have you "speak to the hand" than allow the Holy Spirit to enable me to purr like a spiritual kitten in times of confrontation. What about when the rude driver cuts me off or when my sixteen-year-old challenges me with an exhilarating game of authority tug-of-war? How about when an adult child still living at home won't get a job or lift a finger around the house to help? What happens to gentleness? David Bowie's song "Fill Your Heart" says, "Gentleness clears the soul and love cleans the mind and makes it free!" How did he know that gentleness is good for the mind, the soul, and can actually set people free!

The *self-control* fruit of the Spirit is one I sometimes mix up with self-gratification or selfishness. Laura Branigan in her song "Self Control" says, "You take my self, you take my self control. You got me livin' only for the night. Before the morning comes, the story's told. You take my self, you take my self control." Her song goes on to talk about living in the darkness. How she is a "city light painted girl" in the night. She knows that living like this completely strips her of self-control. The song is written in such a way that you get the feeling that she wishes she could regain some self-control in her life, but she feels hopeless in the night hour that she chooses to dwell in.

If the Holy Spirit lives in us, then why is self-control so hard to illuminate in our lives?

It's sad that many Christians dwell in the same feeling of being stripped of self-control. If the Holy Spirit lives in us, then why is self-control so hard to illuminate in our lives? What's my excuse? You'd think that after all these years of walking with Almighty God and experiencing the supernatural life-style I've grown so accustomed to, out of my being would ooze baskets full of the fruit of the Spirit *self-control* in every situation. Not!

Living my life with the fruit of the Spirit on display continues to be a choice that I must make consciously in every situation in which I find myself. Choice is an action. Every day I must ask God to "sing 'em again" as I move forward and call

Living my life with the fruit of the Spirit on display continues to be a choice that I must make consciously in every situation in which I find myself. Choice is an action.

upon the Holy Spirit to clothe me in His love, joy, peace, patience, goodness, kindness, faithfulness, gentleness, and self-control. I aggressively choose to put on the garments of His character, and I aggressively allow Him to exemplify His fruit of the Spirit in my life.

Pursue the Fruit

The fruit of the Spirit is to be desired and pursued through the work of the Spirit within us like my desire for the cherries in the family orchard. Sometimes we need to seize forcefully the fruit and bring it into our daily situations. No, the fruit won't just automatically manifest in our behavior 100 percent of the time. We must reach out for it, grab it, and apply it as needed throughout the day, the week, the month, and the year as God gives us the light and direction to do so. If

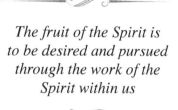

The fruit of the Spirit is to be desired and pursued through the work of the Spirit within us

you are like me, sometimes seizing the fruit of the Spirit and applying it to situations is a moment-by-moment task.

Some of the fruit of the Spirit is easier for me to manifest than others. When I'm in challenging trials, I am more aware of the absence of certain fruit of the Spirit than I am when my situations are less stressful. Out of all the fruit of the Spirit, *kindness* and *peace* seem to be easier for me to display for use on my "life tree." The Lord is developing in me an awareness of people who are struggling with their weaknesses and insecurities. When these weaknesses in character are aimed at me through word curses and petty behaviors, Jesus is able to release kindness toward them through His Spirit within me. As I allow Him to do so, I watch their behaviors change for the better.

What I find with the fruit of the Spirit *love* is that I must go after it quite aggressively through prayer, proclamation, repentance, and dying to myself daily. When I discern through my circumstance that I am lacking love toward others, I begin to pray and ask the Holy Spirit, "Please be love to these people." I begin to proclaim out of my mouth, in a private location or even in a whisper, "I will love you and forgive you, just like Jesus loves and forgives me."

Repentance before God as a regular practice is important in my life. Repentance is not just saying I'm sorry for my sin, but it's an actual turning of the self around from the direction I was going downward and returning to the high place of God's thinking and behaving. Dying to my will to be right, my desire to be important, and my need to be noticed are summed up in dying to myself daily. It takes a combination of prayer, proclamation, and repentance to exact this dying process.

The fruit of the Spirit that is the most challenging for me to expose is joy. Joy is the fruit that I literally have to climb to the top of the tree and grab hold of and make mine every day. I have learned some amazing tools to release joy in my life, especially when depression tries to assault my space. The main tool I've learned to use for releasing joy is laughter.

Just as it is possible to eat without being hungry or drink without being thirsty, so it is with laughter. I have found in my life that I can choose when and what to laugh at. It may seem forced at first, but when you learn how to laugh at the situations in your life or the actions of others that bring pain, either intentionally or unintentionally, there is a genuine joy that gets released. The psalmist has said it best.

"He who sits in the heavens laughs, the Lord scoffs at them."
~Psalm 2:4

In this passage, the laughter that God is releasing into the heavens is not because there's something funny happening on earth. Quite the opposite! The situation is that the nations are raging against Him and His anointed one Jesus. God chooses to laugh at His enemies. It actually says that He scoffs at them.

I have found that when I choose to laugh at the situations that were sent by evil to steal away my joy, something rises up in my soul and strengthens me.

"Then he said to them, 'Go, eat of the fat, drink of the sweet, and send portions to him who has nothing prepared; for this day is holy to our Lord. Do not be grieved, for the joy of the LORD is your strength.'"
~Nehemiah 8:10

Invest, Ingest, Digest, and Manifest

There are four keys to aggressively going after the fruit of the Spirit in your everyday life. These keys will give you an ability to take hold of what is within you by the residence and ongoing work of the Holy Spirit and to administer them in your life situations.

1. *Invest* in a good spiritual "ladder" of prayer. Prayer is simply talking to God with the help of the Holy Spirit in the name and authority of Jesus Christ. As you take time to put your "ladder" up to the tree, or pray to God every day about the fruit of the Spirit and how you desperately want His fruit to influence and change your behavior, He hears you and moves you forward in that direction. Prayer also allows you to reach deeper into the heart of God and open up realms of discernment and revelation of what God feels and thinks.

As you pray, the Holy Spirit is free to begin knitting a warm blanket of truth in you that will allow any frozen part of your heart to melt. Fruit was never meant to be frozen. It tastes the best and carries the most nutrients when it's eaten right off the natural tree. Some of the fruit of the Spirit in you may go dormant for a while, but when you pray, God says to you, "Now is the time to go after the fruit of My Spirit and have it fresh and available in your life. Let the world know that I live within you!"

2. *Ingest* the fruit of the Spirit daily. Accustom yourself to the picking and eating the sweet juice of His fruit. Taste and see how delicious and satisfying He is! Take time to memorize the list of the fruit of the Spirit as recorded in Galatians 5 and savor the flavors (notice the one-syllable, two-syllable, and three-syllabic pattern in the listing: love, joy, peace; patience, goodness, kindness; faithfulness, gentleness, and self-control). The fruit is who God is. As you allow Him to portray His fruit through your life, you find the fruit to be like a delicious seasoning that God sprinkles throughout the entire word of God. Likewise, when you display it, you offer its seasoning to the world.

Each fruit of the Spirit reveals an aspect of the character, personality, and nature of God. As you read the Bible in your daily devotions, make notes as to how many times each fruit of the Spirit is mentioned throughout the Scriptures. Do you know what you will find? How many times is each fruit mentioned? Try this practice and discover the answer for yourself.

3. *Digest* the fruit of the Spirit moment by moment until it becomes so essential in your life that you feel lost and empty without it. Meditate daily on each fruit of the Spirit. Let it

nourish your soul, and watch the Holy Spirit open more doors and opportunities to manifest His presence as you choose to walk in His Spirit. Ask God to reveal to you which fruit of the Spirit that you can display in full force each day. As you move forward in behaving like God, you will grow accustomed to what it feels like to act in His ways when faced with times of testing.

The trademark of reaching maturity as described in this passage is the believers' ability to train (through practice) their senses to discern good from evil (Hebrews 5:14). This truth applies as well to training ourselves through practice in displaying and applying the fruit of the Spirit. It is one of the ways we "take by force" (Matthew 11:12) the fruit of the Spirit. We recognize where we are not liberating it within us and practicing letting it be displayed.

4.   *Manifest* the fruit of the Spirit consistently and at every location in your life. By doing so, you will be letting the world see the very character, personality, and nature of God Himself.

In the trucking or shipping industry, a *manifest* is a list of items on a sheet of paper that are recorded for the driver so he will know what product is to be delivered and where. The driver does not own any of the items on the manifest, but he or his company has been contracted to carry these precious goods to the location agreed upon in the contract. When the driver reaches his destination, he methodically backs his truck into the dock, where the goods are unloaded and successfully relocated.

It's similar to what happens with the fruit of the Spirit. We are merely the vehicles in which this precious nature of God is stored. God through the Holy Spirit is the owner of love, joy, peace, patience, goodness, kindness, faithfulness, gentleness, and self-control. As we allow the Holy Spirit to "unload" Himself through us at each location in our life, we fulfill the manifest. As you let God fulfill His "manifestation" (the fruit of the Spirit) through your life, you experience more and more of His kingdom glory, favor, and abundant life. He is the life, so in essence you experience more of Him as you manifest Him.

> *As you let God fulfill His "manifestation" (the fruit of the Spirit) through your life, you experience more and more of His kingdom glory, favor, and abundant life.*

Fruit Belongs to God

The character, personality, and nature of God, even though they reside in us through the Holy Spirit, do not belong to us. Love, joy, peace, patience, kindness, goodness, faithfulness, gentleness, and self-control are His fruit. God is loving, joyful, and peaceful. We are not so by nature. God is extremely patient, kind, and gentle. We are not. God is altogether good, faithful, and self-controlled. Again, we are not! He displays Himself to the world as the Holy Spirit manifests Himself through us.

> *The fruit of the Spirit is not naturally manifested in us at every moment of every situation we encounter.*

The fruit of the Spirit is not naturally manifested in us at every moment of every situation we encounter. Every day, therefore, it is important to remember each fruit of the Spirit and ask God for its application in our lives. It's when our trials and distresses are the greatest that we are in desperate need for the Holy Spirit to make His fruit available.

The idea of looking at God as the One who is mad at the world because of sin and wants to bring judgment and calamity upon people because they don't repent needs to be revisited. Since the fruit of the Spirit does not reflect anger, judgment, hatred, or wrath, how can we think God's character and nature does? The Scripture does say that God has reserved "the day of wrath." There will be a day when sin will be judged again, just as it was judged upon the cross through the blood of His Son Jesus the first time. Those who receive His Son Jesus and the forgiveness that He brought through the cross will be "saved" from this, the day of wrath. This is Truth, the Good News!

"Or do you think lightly of the riches of His kindness and tolerance and patience, not knowing that the kindness of God leads you to repentance? But because of your stubbornness and unrepentant heart you are storing up wrath for yourself in the day of wrath and revelation of the righteous judgment of God, who WILL RENDER TO EACH PERSON ACCORDING TO HIS DEEDS." ~Romans 2:4-6 (emphasis mine)

We can see in this passage that God is rich in kindness, tolerance, and patience; and it's the "kindness of God that leads you to repentance." Does God like sin? No. Does God love people? Yes. Does God take pleasure in the wicked dying? No! See His words here.

"Say to them, 'As I live!' declares the Lord GOD, 'I take no pleasure in the death of the wicked, but rather that the wicked turn from his way and live. Turn back, turn back from your evil ways! Why then will you die, O house of Israel?'" ~Ezekiel 33:11

Let's reexamine the Scripture and compare it to His character, personality, and nature reflected in the fruit of the Spirit. Let's take to heart from the Romans 2:6 passage, where it is clear that "the riches of His kindness and tolerance and patience" (verse 4) lead us to repentance, and that He has reserved "the day of wrath" (verse 6) to bring final judgment on sin. We must rethink the notion that God would violate His own fruit in dealing with our weakness and sin through death and destruction. God is love, light, and truth. He cannot violate who He is and the power of forgiveness that the blood of His Son released upon the world. And He cannot require us to live in the fruit of the Spirit if He violates His own nature in dealing with mankind. The fruit of the Spirit belongs to God.

> *We must rethink the notion that God would violate His own fruit in dealing with our weakness and sin through death and destruction.*

Fruit Is the Key to Life

Life in the fruit of the Spirit is amazing. It's this life that God requires us to walk in as we grow in the ways of His Kingdom. The key to walking through life in the fruit of the Spirit is to recognize the difference between the attitude of your flesh and the attitude of the Spirit. It's a very simple test. If your behavior at any time is in opposition to the fruit of the Spirit—love, joy, peace, patience, kindness, goodness, faithfulness, gentleness, and self-control—then you are walking in the flesh. The quicker you can recognize the behavior of the flesh and realize you are powerless unless the Spirit of God enters your situation, the faster you are able to walk in the fruit of the Spirit and experience the Kingdom of God in this world.

The key to walking through life in the fruit of the Spirit is to recognize the difference between the attitude of your flesh and the attitude of the Spirit.

Abundant life is ours when we are walking in the fruit of the Spirit. When we fall short of walking in the fruit of the Spirit in situations of our lives, we find ourselves fighting against ourselves just to keep functioning in those things we know to be right. When we don't love, then we find ourselves avoiding the ones that challenge us to love. We fall into a cycle of displaying ungodly, "unfruitful" behavior. Eventually we fall into the snares of the devil and our flesh. The Christian life becomes difficult to maintain, and darkness tends to find places within our souls to torment us. Continuing to walk in the flesh in opposition to the fruit of the Spirit will eventually feed destruction and death into our lives and inevitably erode away our faith, making it impossible to please God.

"And without faith it is impossible to please Him, for he who comes to God must believe that He is and that He is a rewarder of those who seek Him." ~Hebrews 11:6

Fruit Begins at Home

Manifesting the fruit of the Spirit begins at home. It is often easier to have patience at the workplace, with friends, and with acquaintances than with the family. Why? It's because God ordained the family to represent the relationship that He has with the heavenly Godhead. The Father loves the Son; the Son loves and obeys the Father. The Holy Spirit is the third person of the Godhead that enables this relationship to continue in power and perfection.

In the family, the husband loves the wife and gives himself to her for the sake of communion and sacrifice. The wife respects and sub-mits who she is to the husband for the sake of mutual vision and empowerment. The children obey and honor the parents for the sake of protection and blessing. Of course, the family would be the first place that God would test us in the fruit of the Spirit. When the fruit of the Spirit can be manifested in the everyday life of the family, then the Kingdom of God is more clearly seen in the world.

When the fruit of the Spirit can be manifested in the everyday life of the family, then the Kingdom of God is more clearly seen in the world.

It is hypocrisy when we release the fruit of the Spirit to strangers and friends but fail to do so when we are with our families. Is it any wonder that kids become confused, hurt, and bitter and some fall away from the faith because of our hypocrisy?

While I was preparing for a mission trip to Uganda and Italy with Women with a Mission in 2006, I decided one evening to work on my teaching on the fruit of the Spirit. It was getting late, and I was tired. I was feeling a bit overwhelmed because I had about seven lessons to prepare for that three-week journey. My husband had some things he needed me to do as well, and I quickly found my concentration being pulled from my studies to menial tasks he needed done. "Why now? Can't you see I'm busy?" I snapped.

He persisted on capturing my full attention and service. I lost my train of thought and got very angry, very quickly. We had an argument over the situation, and it was my perception that he just didn't understand how important it was for me to continue my preparations for my trip. In his mind, it was not a big deal that I would take some time and serve him by completing a task for him.

Soon our argument escalated, and I found I needed to leave the house to run from my anger and pain. I got in my car and began to weep before the Lord, asking Him why it was necessary that I drop everything I was doing to attend to something so trivial that could definitely wait another day. As I poured out my heart to Him, driving down Interstate 80 E with no destination in mind, the Lord reminded me that not even one fruit of the Spirit was being manifested in my life at the moment. I quickly argued with Him and said, "Yes, there is. There is self-control, because if there wasn't, then I'd probably be sitting in a jail cell right now being charged with spousal abuse or murder." In other words, I had restrained myself in my anger by not physically hurting anyone. That deserved some kudos, didn't it?

Though I was partly joking with God as I wiped my tears of frustration away, what He said to me was true. There were no visible signs of the fruit of the Spirit in my life at the moment. No amount of mission trips or Bible study could manifest what was so desperately needed in my heart at that time. There was no love, joy, peace, patience, goodness, kindness, faithfulness, gentleness, and very little self-control governing my behavior toward my husband. How could I teach on the subject if I couldn't live it?

I quickly took out my spiritual "ladder" of prayer and proclamation, crawled out of my "flesh," and reached high into the tree of the Spirit for the fruit to be released in my life. Just like my hunger for cherries earlier in the chapter required me to put my horse away and get a ladder to reach the fruit on the tree, so it was with my desperate need to reach the *patience* fruit of the Spirit in my life. My spiritual ladder of prayer and proclamation was my ability to call fervently upon the Holy Spirit to unleash the fruit of the Spirit *patience* in my life that moments earlier was out of my reach.

I came to my senses and repented before God for the absence of the fruit of the Spirit *patience* toward my husband, turned the car around, and went home. I humbly apologized to my husband and went about the house, happily helping him with the important task that he needed to have done. I think it was folding the clothes or something like that. Whatever it was, it was important to him at that moment.

Unfortunately, the more we become conscious of the fruit of the Spirit and the role it plays in our lives, the more we are tempted to sell out and walk in the flesh.

Looking back, I wonder if I really was willing to sell my soul over a dryer full of clothes. Unfortunately, the more we become conscious of the fruit of the Spirit and the role it plays in our lives, the more we are tempted to sell out and walk in the flesh—sometimes for less than a dryer full of clothes. May it never be, Lord!

Call upon the Holy Spirit to manifest His fruit through you at any given moment, and you will be struck with awe as to how He begins to transform your situation through His fruit in your life.

Fruit Distinguishes True from False

Much of the global body of Christ walks in a subtle fear of being deceived. Saints don't want to move into the prophetic gifts of God for fear of being deceived by false prophets. Pastors hesitate to allow a free flow of the Holy Spirit in their worship services for fear of false worshipers drawing attention to them and losing control of the congregation. Many people think the answer that will keep them safe is to live on the defensive when it comes to anything that looks overly spiritual or mystical because they fear that the spirit that has true power in these situations is the devil.

When Jesus came on the scene, performing miracles, He was accused of being the "prince of demons" Beelzebul. In the minds of the religious leaders, Jesus' manifestation of power could only be of the devil. Jesus quickly set them straight on where His power came from.

"But when the Pharisees heard this, they said, 'This man casts out demons only by Beelzebul the ruler of the demons.' And knowing their thoughts Jesus said to them, 'Any kingdom divided against itself is laid waste; and any city or house divided against itself will not stand. If Satan casts out Satan, he is divided against himself; how then will his kingdom stand? If I by Beelzebul cast out demons, by whom do your sons cast them out? For this reason they will be your judges. But if I cast out demons by the Spirit of God, then the kingdom of God has come upon you.'" ~Matthew 12:24-28

Jesus explained to His opponents of power that it was very clear how to distinguish the greater power from the lesser. Satan, the devil, could not cast himself out. So the power being manifested was the greater power, the Spirit of God, representing the Kingdom of God. He pointed out that even the religious leaders' "sons and daughters" were casting demons out. Even their children knew the difference between true and false power through the Spirit of God. Because of this experience in the reality of the Kingdom of God's power, these children would one day be judges.

Jesus did warn the disciples against false prophets, but He gave them the "heads- up" on how to recognize them. It would be easy, He said, because of the fruit of the Spirit they manifested in their lives.

"Beware of the false prophets, who come to you in sheep's clothing, but inwardly are ravenous wolves. You will know them by their fruits. Grapes are not gathered from thorn bushes nor figs from thistles, are they? So every good tree bears good fruit, but the bad tree bears bad fruit. A good tree cannot produce bad fruit, nor can a bad tree produce good fruit. Every tree that does not bear good fruit is cut down and thrown into the fire. So then, you will know them by their fruits."
~Matthew 7:15-20

In this Scripture passage, Jesus gives an explanation regarding false prophets that uses trees and fruit. There is a direct correlation, He says, between a tree and its fruit. Jesus refers to two trees: a good tree and a bad tree. And He refers to the fruit as good and bad. Examining the fruit is the way to recognize false prophets from the others.

False prophets come into our midst, disguising themselves as the innocent sheep, but inwardly they are deadly and are looking to destroy. Their fruit is not the behavior of anyone displaying the character, personality, and nature of God. The fruit of the Spirit never looks to destroy but to bring God's life. So like the disciples, you can distinguish true prophets from false prophets by the fruit of the Spirit manifested in their lives.

Prophecy is a gift of the Spirit, and the assignment, or office, of the prophet is God's gift to the church. It is a governmental office that God uses to establish foundation and truth. So there is no need to be fearful of God's governmental gifts if we understand the role that the fruit of the Spirit plays in their validity.

"And He gave some as apostles, and some as prophets, and some as evangelists, and some as pastors and teachers, for the equipping of the saints for the work of service, to the building up of the body of Christ; until we all attain to the unity of the faith, and of the knowledge of the Son of God, to a mature man, to the measure of the stature which belongs to the fullness of Christ." ~Ephesians 4:11-13

The prophet as well as the apostle, evangelist, pastor, and teacher are not exempt from portraying the fruit of the Spirit. God's governmental officials that He gifts to the church are to represent God's heart, mind, and purposes on this earth in all that they say and do. If what they speak is not representing the fruit of the Spirit, then we are to question how "good" the tree is.

God's governmental officials that He gifts to the church are to represent God's heart, mind, and purposes on this earth in all that they say and do.

"Or do you think lightly of the riches of His kindness and tolerance and patience, not knowing that the kindness of God leads you to repentance?" ~Romans 2:4

Here we see that God Himself uses His fruit of the Spirit *kindness* to lead people to repentance. If a prophet, apostle, evangelist, pastor, or teacher thinks that repentance comes any other way than through God's kindness, as clearly stated in His Word, then he or she isn't putting faith in how God works. Those who endeavor to speak for God are required to act as He acts. The fruit of the Spirit *kindness* is a perfect example of the way that God acts—He leads us through His kindness to repentance.

Two Trees: Knowledge or Life?

In the garden of Eden were two trees that God called to the attention of Adam and Eve. One was "the tree of the knowledge of good and evil" and the other one was "the tree of life" (Genesis 2:9). God prohibited Adam and Eve from eating from the tree of the knowledge of good and evil. The one that He wanted them to eat the fruit from was the tree of life. Why?

Is it wrong to know good and evil or the difference between good and evil? I don't think it was what God wanted for Adam and Eve. Knowledge "puffs up" (1 Corinthians 8:1, NRSV); but experiencing love "builds up," or provides humility, fervency, and boldness. The fruit of the tree of knowledge would have made them haughty and proud. In contrast, the fruit of the tree of life (and love) would let them experience more of God and keep His breath surging through their spirits, keeping them in right relationship with Him.

Living in the Kingdom of God is not just knowing about God. It's not just acquiring knowledge about the Bible. It's not even about knowing mysteries and secrets of heaven. Living in the Kingdom of God is experiencing the life of God and knowing Him personally: His person, His ways, and His heart. Experiencing God by knowing Him personally in our lives is the purest form of relationship. The Kingdom

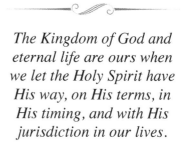

The Kingdom of God and eternal life are ours when we let the Holy Spirit have His way, on His terms, in His timing, and with His jurisdiction in our lives.

of God and eternal life are ours when we let the Holy Spirit have His way, on His terms, in His timing, and with His jurisdiction in our lives.

"This is eternal life, that they may know You, the only true God, and Jesus Christ whom You have sent." ~John 17:3

I once was told by someone who was teaching on the gifts of the Spirit that he only wanted to let God demonstrate His gifts on Wednesday nights after the service was over, during an "afterglow" time. That statement took my breath away, and fear gripped my soul. I went home later that night and repented for the entire body of Christ. How presumptuous to think that God has chosen us to dictate to Him when, where, and how often He is allowed to move by His Spirit in our midst? Hopefully there will come a day when we stop trying to control God's work. May He find freedom in you and me to be who He is—anytime and anywhere!

We live in a culture that reverences knowledge above life experience. God desires a church that hungers and thirsts for all of His fullness to move upon this earth, not one that just knows about it.

Every time we meet together, our first question to God should be, "Lord, how do You want to display Your power in our midst?" Our next statement should be, "Lord, search me and know me and see if there is any wicked way in me." Walking in the fullness of His Spirit requires both of these prayers.

Let's revisit Scripture cited in Chapter One of this book for its applicability here.

"Either make the tree good and its fruit good, or make the tree bad and its fruit bad; for the tree is known by its fruit. You brood of vipers, how can you, being evil, speak what is good? For the mouth speaks out of that which fills the heart. The good man brings out of his good treasure what is good; and the evil man brings out of his evil treasure what is evil. But I tell you that every careless word that people speak, they shall give an accounting for it in the day of judgment. For by your words you will be justified, and by your words you will be condemned." ~Matthew 12:33-37

Here Jesus is addressing the religious leaders of that day, the Pharisees, who have just accused Him of being Beelzebul, the prince of demons, because He cast out a demon from someone. Casting out demons is one of the gifts of the Spirit, referred to in 1 Corinthians 12:10 as "distinguishing of spirits." Jesus firmly rebukes these leaders by implying that their "tree" is bad because they are attributing the work of the Holy Spirit, in this case casting out demons, to be work of the devil. This is clearly an example of a bad tree in action! Their words are evil, their tree is evil, their fruits are evil, and their treasures are evil.

What Jesus is saying is that His true followers never, and I mean never, attribute the work of the Holy Spirit to the work of the devil. When people attribute the gifts of the Holy Spirit to the works of the devil, then Jesus refers to their life, or tree, as bad. Good fruit does not grow on bad trees. Bad trees refer to those that carry the belief system that God is not able to perform His work today through the manifestation of the power of the Holy Spirit. Thankfully, there is forgiveness through repentance in doubting God's purposes and power. Good fruit of the Spirit is essential in displaying God's character on the earth.

"Either make the tree good and its fruit good, or make the tree bad and its fruit bad; for the tree is known by its fruit." ~Matthew 12:33

Every one of us must be "born again" of the Spirit, as Jesus speaks about to Nicodemus, the Pharisee.

"Jesus answered and said to him, 'Truly, truly, I say to you, unless one is born again he cannot see the kingdom of God.'" ~John 3:3

If you have confessed Jesus Christ as your Lord, put your faith in the God of the Bible, and allowed the Holy Spirit to possess and fill you, then you are considered a good tree destined to mature and produce the good fruit of the Spirit.

If you have confessed Jesus Christ as your Lord, put your faith in the God of the Bible, and allowed the Holy Spirit to possess and fill you, then you are considered a good tree destined to mature and produce the good fruit of the Spirit.

Let your roots of faith be attached to the good Vine, Jesus Christ. Let these roots go deep into the good soil of your soft heart, where there is no room for darkness or deceit. Let the armor of God, your righteousness, protect you as you advance in Kingdom victory over temptation and sin. As you receive your nourishment from the Holy Spirit and the Word of God, then your fruit will be good; it will be the fruit of the Spirit. You will find yourself discerning more and more when your behavior is contrary to His fruit. And your hunger for His life in you will cause you to desire aggressively to release His fruit in your everyday life.

> *As you receive your nour-ishment from the Holy Spirit and the Word of God, then your fruit will be good; it will be the fruit of the Spirit.*

Time to Pray

If you would like the Heavenly Father to make you more aware of the fruit of the Spirit being displayed in your life and help you grow in them, please pray this prayer.

"Father God, I come to You in Jesus' name, and I thank you for opening my eyes to the need to bear the "good fruit" of the Spirit in my life. Show me how I can continue to make my tree good and grow in the fruit of the Spirit in all areas of my life. In Jesus' name, amen."

Time to Apply

Turn to Chapter Two in your *Life Enhancement Journal* at the back of the book, and ask God how He would have you apply these truths to your life. When you have completed the exercise, move forward to Chapter Three: *God Is LOVE.*

Chapter Three

God Is LOVE

*L*ove, in the world of human emotion, is often understood as a feeling that promotes happiness, well-being, and pleasure. The word is used interchangeably and very loosely to express feelings toward people, animals, food, events, and entertainment: "I love you. I love that guy. I love puppies. I love bananas and peanut butter. I love parades. I love movies. I love wrestling matches. I love chick flicks! I love vacations. I love music. I love football. I love Jesus."

The kingdom of this world and the Kingdom of God define love differently. The kingdom of this world defines *love,* according to *Webster's Dictionary,* as a feeling, a great enjoyment, or the result of a warm emotion, that which brings great pleasure and satisfaction and preference. Even though a portion of society is capable of altruistic love (serving communities through volunteering services, time, and money to help the needy), human love, especially when linked to relationships between one another, is conditional and limited to self-gratification and promotion.

Self-gratification and promotion in love speak for themselves when we take a look at divorce statistics, abandonment of children, disposing of unwanted pregnancies, and infidelity in relationships. Human love has been reduced for the most part to that which is convenient and self-serving and offers promotion of its own wants and needs. As long as the person or object being loved is affecting the one who loves in a positive way, then that person or object earns the right to remain in the heart of the one who loves. But when inconvenience, confrontation, boredom, or threat to personal needs happens, then the "love" is affected negatively and shifts in other directions.

Human love (that which is not from God's Spirit), because of its self-agenda, is susceptible to leaving a trail of pain in people's lives. Violent acts that accompany jealousy, fits of rage, and many criminal behaviors are often said to be done "in the name of love." As perverted as this reasoning is to society, in the mind of the perpetrator, "love" was the reason for the crime.

Agape Love

The love that is fruit of the Spirit in God's Kingdom is best defined by the Greek word *agape*. This Greek version of the word *love* is used in many places in Scripture where the word *love* appears. The biblical use of *agape* love means to communicate affection, goodwill, benevolence, charity, and self-sacrificing actions. *Agape* love usually refers to actions toward another person without sexual implication involved; however, it can be applied in the sexual union as well in those times when we prefer our spouse's needs above our own needs.

> Agape *love compels us to behave without any expectance of receiving a reward.*

Agape love compels us to behave without any expectance of receiving a reward. *Agape* love is completely void of tactics of manipulation and control. Everything done out of *agape love* fruit of the Spirit is done to benefit someone else, even to the point of sacrificing one's needs.

The kingdom of this world measures its love according to how the one showing love is affected, but the Kingdom of God measures its *agape love* fruit of the Spirit according to how it affects others. As seen in our Lord Jesus Christ in regard to relationship toward us and His Father, Jesus' acts of *agape* love exemplify self-sacrifice. Sacrificing His life to bring us into relationship with His Father and Creator of the world is the perfect picture of *agape love* fruit of the Spirit. This *agape love* fruit of the Spirit transcends our ability to give our time and money to charity; but it reaches deep into our ability to sacrifice our wants, needs, and emotions in order serve and prefer others above ourselves. In fact, this *agape love* fruit of the Spirit is the evidence that points to our true knowledge of God, experiential relationship, and dedication to His purposes.

"Beloved, let us love [agapao] one another, for love [agape] is from God; and everyone who loves [agapao] is born of God and knows God. The one who does not love [agapao] does not know God, for God is love [agape]. By this the love [agape] of God was manifested in us, that God has sent His only begotten Son into the world so that we might live through Him. In this is love [agape], not that we loved [agape] God, but that He loved [agape] us and sent His Son to be the propitiation for our sins. Beloved, if God so loved [agape] us, we also ought to love [agape] one another. No one has seen God at any

time; if we love [agapao] one another, God abides in us, and His love [agape] is perfected in us." ~1 John 4:7-12 (bracketed text mine)

Notice in the original Greek version of 1 John 4:7-12, in addition to *agape*, the use of the Greek word *agapao* also, which is another form of the word *agape*. *Agapao* means to have preference, to wish well or regard the welfare of others. When we come into the Kingdom of God through salvation, Scripture says, we "ought to" extend *agape* love, which includes the larger concept of love as expressed in the word *agapao*.

Giving preference to others over ourselves is an "ought" for us in our display of *agape love* fruit of the Spirit, just as Jesus chose our redemption over His own comfort. But to what extent can this be true for us? To what extent have we truly given or received unconditional love in our own experiences through life? I've personally never been loved by another human being entirely unconditionally, so how am I supposed to know how to love someone else unconditionally?

The inability of humans to *agape* love me was what brought me to the unconditional love of God in the first place. In that instant when I gave my life to God, who is *agape* love, He gave me His Spirit and made me His own. He marked me with the seal of His love, and He expects me to love the human race in the same way He does.

Without the Holy Spirit empowering us to live out the agape love fruit of the Spirit in us, to love others as God loves us is an impossible task.

What is true for me as a child of God about His *agape* love is true for all of us. Without the Holy Spirit empowering us to live out the *agape love* fruit of the Spirit in us, to love others as God loves us is an impossible task. Our lifelong journey of being godly Kingdom dwellers is a relentless mission that has one primary purpose, and that is to turn us into Christ's likeness, which includes being unconditional lovers of God and mankind. God desires to entrust His people with the innate ability to behave in ways toward others that reflect His unconditional benevolence and undeserving charity. So, with that, "let the games begin!"

A friend of mine just recently shared a story with me about how God revealed His love to her in an unexpected way. Judgments were the minefield that she had walked in and struggled with for most of her life. The judgments she made about people in their weakness and bondages affected how she would treat them. Contempt and avoidance was a common behavior that she would express toward those who couldn't find victory over the past. In behaving this way, however, she heightened the insecurities she felt in herself.

My friend told me of a woman she was acquainted with at her church. The woman seemed always to dwell in the skin of her past. When my friend would try to get close to her, the woman, out of her pain and hurt, would not allow herself to develop a close friendship. My friend's past life had been difficult as well, but she had learned to deal with it. Why couldn't this woman just "get over it"? Why did their friendship have to be constantly threatened?

One Sunday in worship service, my friend looked over at this sister in Christ and clearly felt a signal from God in her spirit to keep her judgmental "hands off." She heard the voice of God speak to her and say, "She's mine. I love her." As she listened to these words from God, she could feel His incredible love for this wounded, broken soul. For several months after that time, every time my friend saw this woman, she could hear the words repeated from heaven, "She's mine. I love her."

My friend testifies today that hearing God's words of love for this woman began the wonderful journey of being freed from a judgmental spirit and moving deeper into the loving heart of God for herself and for others. She exchanged judgments for the freedom to love. This change in her happened through a revelation of God's *agape love* fruit of the Spirit released in her heart and her mind for this woman.

What Does *Agape Love* Fruit Look Like?

Agape love is the experiential character of God. Not only is it God's character shown forth in actions toward others, but it is God Himself. God is love! It is His benevolent love that sent Jesus to the earth. It is His charitable compassion that caused Jesus to heal sickness; raise the dead; and take the beatings, mocking, and scourging. It is the unconditional love of God that continues giving, even today, while we continue taking. He continues forgiving while we continue sinning. He continues blessing while we continue in our failings, complaining, and selfishness.

> Agape *love is the experiential character of God.*

The image of God reflects loving the world unconditionally, and He wants us to be the reflection of His image — not only for His sake but for ours. He desires that we too become givers of benevolent and charitable love in all situations and to all people in our life. He wants His bride, those who have put their trust in Him, to have all the spots of distrust and skepticism and the wrinkles of jealousy, bitterness, and resentment removed from their love garments of righteousness.

The qualities of *agape* love and evidence of it are many. Scripture describes them for us using very concrete words.

"Love is patient, love is kind and is not jealous; love does not brag and is not arrogant, does not act unbecomingly; it does not seek its own, is not provoked, does not take into account a wrong suffered, does not rejoice in unrighteousness, but rejoices with the truth; bears all things, believes all things, hopes all things, endures all things. Love never fails. . . . But now faith, hope, love, abide these three; but the greatest of these is love." ~1 Corinthians 13:4-8a, 13

Since *agape* love is fruit of the Spirit living in us, then we know that the Spirit is able to be all these love qualities in us. Every one of us would do well to memorize the love attributes in this Scripture passage and match them against every bit of behavior toward every person in our lives at all times. If we did so, we would spend our lives attempting to perfect the outward display of His love toward the people in our lives.

At the end of every encounter with a human being, it is a good idea to analyze our love meters with these questions: Was I patient? Was I kind? Did I brag? Did I seek my own way? Did I get provoked? Am I keeping an account of wrong that this person has done against me? If the answer is yes to any of these questions at any time about anyone, then it's time to call on the Holy Spirit within to release His *love* fruit in a greater measure in our lives.

The *love* fruit of the Spirit is listed first in the list of fruit of the Spirit in the Scripture because it's the first link in the chain of God's character qualities. Love links to joy, peace, patience, kindness, good-

ness, faithfulness, gentleness, and self-control. Love begins the chain, and it can bring about a chain reaction in our life, allowing the rest of the fruit and character of God to flow. Show me someone who lacks love in a situation, and I'll show you someone lacking in the rest of the fruit of the

The love *fruit of the Spirit is listed first in the list of fruit of the Spirit in the Scripture because it's the first link in the chain of God's character qualities.*

Spirit. This is why the greatest of the three—faith, hope, and love—is love.

They Will Know We Belong to Jesus by Our Love

Before the Passover supper began, Jesus wanted to set an example and show the disciples what charitable love looked like. He set aside His own garments and began washing the disciples' feet. When He came to Peter's feet, Peter refused to have Him wash them. Peter, probably feeling very humble and religious in his zealous refusal, said to Jesus, "Never shall you wash my feet." Jesus patiently took the time to explain to him that if he didn't let Him wash his feet, then Peter could not be a part of Him. Reluctantly, Peter allowed Jesus to wash his feet, an act of unconditional love by Jesus, without any expectation of Peter to return the service to Him.

After the foot washing ceremony, Jesus began to serve His disciples the Passover dinner. His act of love again was unconditional toward them, never expecting them to serve Him dinner in return. He then pointed to His actions as examples of *agape* love.

"By this all men will know that you are My disciples, if you have love for one another." ~John 13:35

Jesus knew that unconditional love was a completely foreign concept to these men because they had been taught to act according to the Jewish law, "An eye for an eye and a tooth for a tooth," which was clearly a mindset of judgment and retribution. It was important for the disciples to understand the power of the new *agape* love, which would be the unique and distinctive trademark of the new covenant between God and man.

Jesus was telling them that the way the world would look upon them, as being His followers, would be because they carried within their hearts and demonstrated in their lives this unconditional and benevolent love for each other. This love would look different from the way the followers of the Jewish law would act toward one another. It would be the love that would distinguish them and prove that they belonged to God through faith in Jesus Christ.

During one of the visits to the Mount of Olives, the disciples asked Him to reveal more about the signs of the "end of the age." It was in this context that Jesus spoke more about the power that unconditional love would make on the world.

"Then they will deliver you to tribulation, and will kill you, and you will be hated by all nations because of My name. At that time many will fall away and will betray one another and hate one another. Many false prophets will arise and will mislead many. Because lawlessness is increased, most people's love will grow cold. But the one who endures to the end, he will be saved." ~Matthew 24:9-13

When the end of the age is in full force, with hatred and betrayal of one another being prevalent, when sin and lawlessness have increased greatly, then the kind of love that the kingdom of this world knows about would grow cold. Enduring in unconditional love, the *love* fruit of the Spirit, however, would insure their salvation.

Let me bring this point closer to home. When all the love around you is growing cold and there is no *agape* love coming your way, if you can stay in benevolent and charitable devotion to one another, without expecting anything in return, you will be saved. Saved from what? In the context of Matthew 24:9-13, you will be saved from "falling away" and being "misled by many." Your *agape* love toward others will keep you strong in your faith and prove that you belong to God.

> *Your* agape *love toward others will keep you strong in your faith and prove that you belong to God.*

Talking with God

Knowing how important it is to remain in the unconditional love of God, I set my mind to seek understanding for statements such as "those who endure to the end will be saved." In my prayer time, I said, "Father, please talk to me more about agape love." I waited for His response, and as soon as I heard Him speak, I began to write what I heard. Here is what I heard the Father in heaven say to me about *agape* love.

My *agape* love is always serene. It does not strive; it has no fear. I am the purest love, and I am always in control with My love. Because I am love, I never worry. I don't worry about ever having or being enough for you. I am love; therefore, I am everything. I was before there was anything. All the power that resides in Me you have not known, nor have you ever seen. Love is My power. What you see all came from love, and what you don't see resides in My love. My love is perfect obedience to what is right.

All righteousness comes from love. I established the heavens in righteousness through My love. When My Son Jesus took on the form of human flesh to be like you, He put on the cloak of love, which is perfect obedience and righteousness to the end. My love was in Him. His love for Me caused Him to give His life up to death, even death on the cross. People say that no one put Him there, but I say love put Him there and kept Him there so you could one day know this love.

It was love that rose Him from the dead and continues to hold all power over death. Do you see now why the greatest of these—hope, faith, and love—is love? It is because I am love, and I am the greatest.

I responded to God by saying, "I see You are the greatest and that You are love. I see that Your love covers my sin through the death and resurrection blood of Your Son. I know that Your love lives in me through the fruit of Your Holy Spirit, but Father, I still fail at loving unconditionally. How can Your love be perfected in me? I don't want anything less than pure love for mankind just like You do. Not because mankind deserves it, but because You want to have a people that You call direct descendants of Your *agape* love who share and express Your *agape* love to this world. My desire is for You to be so magnified in me that my heart yearns to reflect Your love the way You originally intended it."

Words from the Lord came to me a second time. Here is what I heard.

> I will perfect agape love in you as you yield to every opportunity. Learn what love is. My Spirit will dwell in you and move you into new realms and opportunities to love the unlovely. Do not fear, because perfect love casts out all fear. My Spirit has not given you a spirit of fear but of explosive power, unconditional love, and a complete and whole mind, which is the mind of Christ.
>
> Love is giving without expectant return. I will perfect you through opportunities to give, knowing that you will never get paid back. I will open doors for you to give of your time, your money, and your emotional support, knowing that those people who receive from you may not ever give back to you the same. I will give you a heart of benevolence and opportunity to put others first above yourself, all the while knowing that they will not be able to return the same sacrifice to you as you gave to them.
>
> Now that you hunger and thirst for My *agape* love, I will perfect this fruit of My Spirit in you. Manifesting My pure love is best released in unlovely and unloving situations. Just stay focused on Me.

Memorize what love is in 1 Corinthians 13 so that you will be able to measure your growth in every situation.

My conversation with the Father didn't end there. "Father, talk to me about opportunities to show *agape* love to the world," I said. "I feel like I fail most of the time."

He then said to me:

Opportunity comes in all shapes and sizes. There are great opportunities to show benevolent and charitable love in this world. The best times are in intense persecution and ridicule for your faith. There are also friendly opportunities to show My love within your own family, your husband, your son, your sisters, brothers, mother, and father.

The family is the hardest place to love unconditionally due to the high expectations you place on family members. The damage of disappointment throughout the years has festered in layers of past hurts, bitterness, resentment, and unforgiveness. Unconditionally loving your own family is the most challenging because of the level of familiarity between each member. They know you so well and they are most likely to ridicule your thoughts and opinions about our relationship and what you do for Me or how I choose to work in your life. If you can master *agape* love in your own family, then loving the world unconditionally will be much easier.

Before I sent My Son Jesus to love you unconditionally, We—the Holy Spirit, Jesus, and I—shared
love with each other. We are the original family.
We have always been before any of creation came
into existence. Our love for each other caused Us to
create you so you could share in Our bountiful love.
It's because of My Son's *agape* love for Me and the
Holy Spirit that He agreed to die for you. It was love
that compelled Him to obey and become that love
on the cross so you could share Our love together.
So, first focus on opportunities for love within your
own family, then your friends, then your coworkers,
then the strangers on the street, and then the world
and other nations. When *agape* love for your family
is perfected, then *agape* love will spill into all areas
of your life.

"Father I am so sorry that I fail the *agape* test at home over and
over again," I said with sad repentance.

His final words to me were life changing:

That's okay. You are forgiven, now you see. A year
ago you did not see; you were blind to many opportunities to *agape* love. Charitably love those in your
own families. Start there and you will find victory in
the other realms of your life. Though a man may fall
seven times I will pick him up. You are changed from
glory to glory. Move forward. Write what you learn

and watch victory come in the mornings and new seasons of your life.

Agape Love Starts at Home

Wow, benevolent love right in our own families? The hardest place to exercise unconditional love *is* in the conflicts at home, and God knows there are many. So many expectations, so many opportunities to forgive, all the while faced with the numerous challenges to act unbecomingly, without patience, boastful, and rude. If I could have a dime for every time I demanded my own way in my family, I'd be completely debt free.

"Above all, keep fervent in your love for one another, because love covers a multitude of sins." ~1 Peter 4:8

Fervent, unconditional love is said to cover a multitude of sins. How can my patience, kindness, not bragging, not boasting, not being arrogant, not acting unbecomingly, not seeking my own, not being easily provoked, not take into account a wrong suffered, not rejoicing in unrighteousness but rejoicing with the truth, bearing all things, believing all things, hoping all things, enduring all things, and never failing cover a multitude of sins?

There is a supernatural anointing that God has placed upon each characteristic of *agape* love. When situations of confrontation and opposition come face-to-face with *agape* love, an anointing of God's transforming power is released. A powerful flow of the forgiveness and conviction of the righteousness of God is made known to all who are present. Since God is complete, unconditional love, and since

Jesus moved in this love and power, doesn't it make sense that our display of *agape* love can make a way for the same power to bring restoration in relationships and situations, both to one another and to God? Love will bring conviction of sin, forgiveness, and eventually eternal life in the lives of those who encounter God through us in this way.

"So, as those who have been chosen of God, holy and beloved, put on a heart of compassion, kindness, humility, gentleness and patience; bearing with one another, and forgiving each other, whoever has a complaint against anyone; just as the Lord forgave you, so also should you. Beyond all these things put on love, which is the perfect bond of unity." ~Colossians 3:12-14

Agape love covers a multitude of sins and is the perfect bond of unity. It is the blanketing effect of this love that tells sinners that there is a way to be free from the sin that separates them from their creator God. Its adhesive effect attaches them to God's redemption and makes them one with Him.

When you move away from unconditional love, you move away from God Himself, for God is agape *love.*

Let us endeavor to wrap ourselves in and around *agape* love. Let's all memorize what love is as described in 1 Corinthians 13, not just putting it into our minds but also into our hearts, and then use it as a checklist in every area of our lives, starting with our own families. Ask the Holy Spirit to quicken your spirit when you find yourself veering from perfect love. When you move away from unconditional love, you move away from God Himself, for God is *agape* love.

Time to Pray

If you would like more of the fruit of the Spirit *love* in your life, pray this prayer.

"Father in heaven, I want you to show more of Your agape *love in me starting with my family and reaching out to the world. Help me to memorize what love is as it is explained in 1 Corinthians 13. Give me the discernment to know when I am called upon to show Your agape love in my situations every day. In Jesus' name, amen."*

Time to Apply

Take some time and ask God in your *Life Enhancement Journal* at the back of the book, about your ability to display His fruit of the Spirit *agape love* in all situations in your life. Be sure not to rush through this exercise, because *agape* love is one of God's favorite subjects! When you have completed this section of your *Life Enhancement Journal*, then turn to Chapter Four: *The JOY of the Lord is Your Strength.*

Chapter Four

The JOY of the Lord Is Your Strength

*T*his world offers a myriad of opportunities to live in despair, hopelessness, and turmoil. Economic instability, hatred, wars, killings, sickness, and death are just a few reasons to justify a life without joy. The human body, through sin and degradation, has slowly been deteriorating. Much of the depression in the world is caused by hormonal imbalances and deficiencies in the body's God-given ability to cope through serotonin and dopamine levels. Is it any wonder that people live joyless lives?

Pharmaceutical companies make millions of dollars offering to the world antidepressants, which in their own right are a wonderful way to regain synthetically some ability to find joy in the good things of life. In no way will I ever denounce the benefits of the human body receiving help to regain, through modern medicine, the ability to function at its highest chemical balance. A lot of sadness and depression comes from hormonal and serotonin imbalances in our deteriorating bodies, but we also must recognize that the devil, our enemy, preys upon these weaknesses.

In the midst of all of these depressing circumstances, there is still good news. The Good News of Jesus Christ brings to each of us the hope and promise of both inner healing and mental healing. This healing comes through the *joy* fruit of the Spirit, which resides in each of us as we allow the Holy Spirit to live and reflect His *joy* fruit through us.

Ironically, addictions to destructive behaviors such as alcoholism, drugs, sex, and other compulsions, including even some serial crimes, are all ways of "self-medication" for the brain to feel a sense of joy and well-being. Joy is a universal craving for every human being. Without some form of joy in our lives, life is hardly worth living. Joy is a basic human need like eating, drinking, and breathing.

The Bible has a lot to say about joy. The *joy* fruit of the Spirit is one of the most powerful forces in the universe, and it is used as a chief weapon to destroy the oppression of the devil in our lives. If it were not so, the devil would not work so hard to debilitate and emotionally paralyze us with grief and sadness.

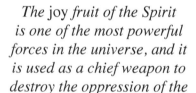

The joy *fruit of the Spirit is one of the most powerful forces in the universe, and it is used as a chief weapon to destroy the oppression of the devil in our lives.*

In the Kingdom of God, as represented in heaven, there is no sadness, despair, or depression. Instead, there is joy. Even though God's heart continues to break for the lost, His joy resounds throughout heaven because He knows that His Son Jesus made provision for every human being to be restored to Him.

We are called to bring the will of God in heaven to this earth, as Jesus taught His disciples to pray, "Your will be done on earth as it is in heaven" (Matthew 6:9-10). He tells us in His Word that the

Kingdom of God on this earth is now "at hand" (Mark 1:15), and the Kingdom of God has "come upon you" (Matthew 12:28 and Luke 11:20). The redeemed of the Lord have been given a mandate, which is to bring the joy of God from heaven to this earth. His joy is our strength (Nehemiah 8:10). His *joy* fruit of the Spirit is available to the body of Christ here on the earth to each of us through the Holy Spirit to strengthen, heal, and establish His dominion over darkness in our lives and the lives of those around us.

Joy: The Force That Enabled Jesus to Endure the Cross

Like *love* fruit, *joy* fruit can be a challenge to manifest consistently every day. That is because the *joy* fruit of the Spirit is unlike any feeling that can be obtained through a drug or natural circumstance, but only through the Holy Spirit within us. Like all other fruit of the Spirit, joy is not feeling-based but attitudinal and is in direct correlation to the transforming of our minds as we learn to think like God thinks. To better understand *joy* fruit, we must look at its biblical definition. The biblical word in Greek for *joy* fruit is *chara*. This word means cheerful, calm, delight, gladness, and inner strength of assurance. *Chara* is the opposite of gloom and depression. God has available to each one of us His supernatural *[chara]* joy when we are in the midst of trials and hardships. An inner strength is within each child of God, from the Holy Spirit, to have calm, delight, and a cheerful and glad demeanor even in extreme turmoil.

Remember the fruit tree analogy? Like all other fruit of the Spirit, *joy* fruit is available at anytime to be seized and forcefully plucked from the spiritual tree of your inner being. The *joy* fruit has nothing to do with outward circumstances. That is why we can consider it all joy when we encounter various trials (James 1:2, KJV). The apostle Paul could share the *joy* fruit of the Spirit, even when he was being "poured out as a drink offering" for his faith (Philippians 2:17). This *joy* fruit is completely motivated by the joy that is in heaven through the Holy Spirit of God.

"Therefore, since we have so great a cloud of witnesses surrounding us, let us also lay aside every encumbrance and the sin which so easily entangles us, and let us run with endurance the race that is set before us, fixing our eyes on Jesus, the author and perfecter of faith, who for the joy set before Him endured the cross, despising the shame, and has sat down at the right hand of the throne of God."
~Hebrews 12:1-2

Knowing that He was to face the shame of sin for the entire world by dying on the cross, Jesus kept His eyes on the "joy set before Him." What joy was this? What was "set before Him"? The throne of God was set before Him. Knowing that in spite of what He was going through or facing, Jesus saw the location of His joy, which was at the right hand of His Father, ruling and reigning in heaven. He knew that in spite of the shame and rejection that He was to undergo and take upon Himself because of sin, He was the heir of a greater, promised inheritance. This inheritance was joy from heaven that would be His eternally.

It was because of this joy from heaven that belonged to Him through His obedience to the Father that Jesus was able to complete His gruesome mission of enduring the cross and satisfying His Father's judgment on sin once and for all. If anyone had a reason to be depressed, it was Jesus. If anyone deserved to numb His emotions through the hyssop and vinegar drink offered to Him at the time of death, it was Jesus. Yet it was because of the joy set before Him that Jesus was able to endure the cross, despising the shame.

Do you find it interesting that it was joy, not love or peace or patience, that was the force from heaven that caused Jesus to move forward in obedience?

Joy: A Mark of the Kingdom

The institution of religion has tried to convince the world that in order to please God, people must adhere to a list of dos and don'ts. Rules, regulations, and traditions of man have been put in place for us to follow if we ever hope to be accepted by God and make it into heaven. Ridicule, punishment, and shame have infiltrated the institution of the church and have been projected toward those who fail or fall short in adhering to the list of church commandments. Jesus, when He came to the earth, redefined what pleased God and what would make mankind acceptable to God.

"For the kingdom of God is not eating and drinking, but righteousness and peace and joy [chara] in the Holy Spirit. For he who in this way serves Christ is acceptable to God and approved by men." ~Romans 14:17-18 (bracketed text mine)

"Joy in the Holy Spirit" is the acceptable way to serve Christ on the earth and please the Father. Notice that eating and drinking has nothing to do with serving God acceptably. What you wear, who you know, and where you go is not what approves you to God. These things do not mark you as a follower of Christ. Like righteousness, and peace, *joy* fruit is a mark of those who are God's children.

Just as He has with *love* fruit, the Holy Spirit has made *chara joy* fruit of the Spirit available to you at all times. It is the second link next to the love link on the chain of the fruit of the Spirit that connects us to the Father. Notice that *peace* fruit is also mentioned as a mark of the Kingdom. Righteousness, peace, and joy in the Holy Spirit set you apart from the kingdom of this world and reflect what the image of God looks like.

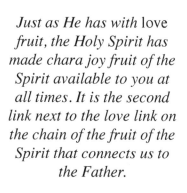

Just as He has with love *fruit, the Holy Spirit has made chara joy fruit of the Spirit available to you at all times. It is the second link next to the love link on the chain of the fruit of the Spirit that connects us to the Father.*

Joy: The Eternal Power Within

In John 16, Jesus spends time with the disciples explaining to them what it will be like when He "goes away." He speaks of His ascension back into heaven after His crucifixion and resurrection. Jesus realizes that sorrow has entered their hearts and tells them the truth about the Holy Spirit and His final role that He will play in their hearts.

"But because I have said these thinwgs to you, sorrow has filled your heart. But I tell you the truth, it is to your advantage that I go away; for if I do not go away, the Helper will not come to you; but if I go, I will send Him to you. . . . Therefore you too have grief now; but I will see you again, and your heart will rejoice, and no one will take your joy [chara] away from you." ~John 16:6-7, 22 (bracketed text mine)

Jesus felt so strongly about this message to His disciples that He repeats the same thing to them fifteen verses later.

"Therefore you too have grief now; but I will see you again, and your heart will rejoice, and no one will take your joy [chara] away from you." ~John 16:22 (bracketed text mine)

He understood that they had not yet had the Holy Spirit living in them to fill them with the *chara joy* fruit of the Spirit. The only joy that the disciples were able to experience up to this point in their relationship with each other and with God was completely based on the outward experiences in their life. When things were good, they had joy; when things weren't good, they were discouraged, confused, sad, and doubtful.

The reason Jesus could say twice in the same discourse that there will be a day when "no one will take your joy away from you" is because He knew that when He would rise from the dead, they would see Him in His resurrection power and victory. He knew that they would receive the Holy Spirit to live within them, and the Spirit would fill them with the supernatural joy *[chara]* that came right from heaven. From then on, nothing could happen on the earth to them or around them that would have the power to "de-possess" them of the availability of the *joy* fruit of the Spirit. This joy would be the power that would sustain them through any persecution, tribulation, or outward circumstance that came against them.

Years later, the apostle Paul proves Jesus' words to be true when he commends the Corinthian church with confidence.

"Great is my confidence in you; great is my boasting on your behalf. I am filled with comfort; I am overflowing with joy [chara] in all our affliction." ~2 Corinthians 7:4 (bracketed text mine)

Even amidst all of his "afflictions," Paul expresses the overflowing *chara joy* fruit that possesses his spirit. Not only does *joy* fruit rule in him, but comfort is his closest companion as well. What fills him? It is the Holy Spirit's comfort and *joy* fruit. The inner strength of this assurance is where his great confidence came from; cheerfulness, calm delight, and gladness were all working in him during his times of great persecution for his faith.

The same sentiments ring through the voice of James, the brother of Jesus, when he writes to the saints regarding their testings, trials, and persecutions for their faith.

"Consider it all joy [chara], my brethren, when you encounter various trials, knowing that the testing of your faith produces endurance. And let endurance have its perfect result, so that you may be perfect and complete, lacking in nothing." ~James 1:2-4 (bracketed text mine)

Basically James exhorts the brethren that are undergoing trials and affliction to let the *joy* fruit of the Spirit have full reign in their hearts because the tests that they are going through will give opportunity for their faith to produce more evidence of "endurance," or patience, which is another fruit of the Spirit. When *patience* fruit of the Spirit is being exercised in their lives, there will be a perfect result. The perfect result will be completeness and lack for nothing.

Again, here is another brick in the building block of God's reflected image, another link in the character quality chain of God's perfection in our lives. It's the *joy* fruit in our trials that allows the *patience* fruit to "have its perfect result." What perfect result is meant here? The perfect result of completeness. To be made complete means to allow the full fruit of the Spirit to have complete reign in our life.

It is inevitable that we encounter various trials in our lives. We have to, because these trials are where we get to know our God better. If there were no trials, there would be no reason to believe that He is able to deliver us. A day will come when there will be no more trials. That day will be awesome. It will be when we are living in heaven with Him. But until then, it is the Holy Spirit's job to comfort us, to lead us into truth, to guide us in the ways of Jesus, and to help us with the tasks for which we are commissioned. The *joy* fruit of the Spirit is an awesome power to release in our lives because it gives us inner strength of assurance to overcome the trials, tribulations, and temptations victoriously.

> *The* joy *fruit of the Spirit is an awesome power to release in our lives because it gives us inner strength of assurance to overcome the trials, tribulations, and temptations victoriously.*

Joy: Brings Spiritual Advancement

As we walk with God in this world and undergo growth through testings, it is God's will that we are constantly advancing and moving forward in His strength and authority. As the *joy* fruit becomes more evident in our lives, we will watch our victories come easier and quicker.

The battles in our lives are not always brought on by the devil, but many times by the way we react to the conflicts and confrontations toward other people, the disappointments and the delusions in our own thinking toward the way things should be going in our lives. When *joy* fruit is perfected through times of misunderstanding, disappointment, conflict, and confrontation, a power from heaven will be released in our midst to clear the way for victory in these areas and other areas to come.

"In this you greatly rejoice, even though now for a little while, if necessary, you have been distressed by various trials, so that the proof of your faith, being more precious than gold which is perishable, even though tested by fire, may be found to result in praise and glory and honor at the revelation of Jesus Christ; and though you have not seen Him, you love Him, and though you do not see Him now, but believe in Him, you greatly rejoice with joy [chara] inexpressible and full of glory, obtaining as the outcome of your faith the salvation of your souls." ~1 Peter 1:6-9 (bracketed text mine)

It is by rejoicing in your trials and aggressively going after the *joy* fruit of the Spirit that you will advance into the heavenly realm of glory and victory, "obtaining as the outcome of your faith the salvation of your souls." *Joy* fruit, when allowed to be evident in your life, disperses the realm of darkness, allowing God's light to shine in to set your freedom in motion. This freedom is the ability to laugh, dance, worship, and proclaim truth even in the midst of your hardest tribulation.

> Joy *fruit, when allowed to be evident in your life, disperses the realm of darkness, allowing God's light to shine in to set your freedom in motion.*

The Holy Spirit is waiting for you to allow Him to be *joy* fruit through you. He wants to give you that inner strength and assurance, that gladness of heart and cheerful, calm delight in spite of the chaos around you.

"Now may the God of hope fill you with all joy [chara] and peace in believing, so that you will abound in hope by the power of the Holy Spirit." ~Romans 15:13 (bracketed text mine)

This verse says you will begin to experience *joy* fruit in your life as you look to the supernatural joy of the "God of hope." Heaven's joy in you is not dependent upon your happy outward circumstances but upon God's very own joy in Him. God's joy, when manifested in your life, will advance you into the supernatural realm of His victorious Kingdom. You will begin to see evidence of miracles in your life, and you will walk with His cheerful and calm delight over you.

Joy: Comes from Hearing the Bridegroom's Voice

In my middle to late 30s, I suffered from a low serotonin level in my brain that launched me into a severe chemical depression. I noticed that when I was in the "dark mental hole," it was hard for me to hear God's voice or to believe that He loved me. The doctor put me on antidepressants, and over time they helped me relate to God in a positive and faithful way. When my imbalances were corrected through the marvels of modern medicine, I was able to progress once again in my faith in His love and will for my life.

About five years into coping with this condition, I left for a three-week mission trip to the Philippines. After six hours on the fourteen-hour plane flight, I realized that I had left my medication at home. Panic began to grip my spirit because I knew that after even one day without my medication, I would begin to sink into the "pit" of depression. Once I was there, the devil would have a mental heyday with me because he would fill my head and heart with lies about people and my God. Because I didn't have the natural or synthetic chemicals in my brain to know better or cope with these lies, he would gain a stronghold against my faith and begin to torment me.

The minute I felt panic hit my heart, I cried out to God on the plane. "Oh God, You have to heal me. I am going overseas to teach about Your love and Your faith. If You allow this physical condition to debilitate my ability to think straight, then I won't be able to accomplish my mission for You." As I prayed in earnest, I felt a peace come over my heart, and I knew that He had heard my cry.

Three days later, after I had been ministering the gospel to the Filipinos, I realized that I had been filled with joy. I never again suffered from depression. I was completely healed. I went for three weeks on that trip without one antidepressant pill and experienced the supernatural joy of God the entire time. I woke up in the mornings happy and went to bed ecstatic over the victories of the day.

On the plane home, I prayed again and told God that I trusted Him to heal me as He had in the Philippines from my clinical depression, and I would trust Him for my life in America. God spoke to my heart and assured me that His joy would be my strength. Hearing His voice filled me with joy even deeper. I felt the words pierce my heart and go deep into the reservoir of my inner being. I knew that the words He spoke to me were my assurance that joy would be mine from that day forth.

"These things I have spoken to you so that My joy [chara] may be in you, and that your joy [chara] may be made full." ~John 15:11 (bracketed text mine)

Jesus mentions in the Scripture that His spoken word would impart His *chara* joy into us and our *chara* joy would be made full.

> *Jesus mentions in the Scripture that His spoken word would impart His chara joy into us and our* chara *joy would be made full.*

Jesus the bridegroom desires to speak to us on a daily basis. The voice of the bridegroom imparts and releases the *joy* fruit of the Spirit that may be lying dormant in our hearts.

"He who has the bride is the bridegroom; but the friend of the bridegroom, who stands and hears him, rejoices greatly because of the bridegroom's voice. So this joy [chara] of mine has been made full." ~John 3:29 (bracketed text mine)

Rejoicing over the bridegroom's voice is the scriptural key in letting the Holy Spirit bring joy in the most difficult situations. I have learned to seek the voice of Jesus, the bridegroom, when I am struggling to release the *joy* fruit of the Spirit.

> *Rejoicing over the bridegroom's voice is the scriptural key in letting the Holy Spirit bring joy in the most difficult situations.*

Joy: Enables Us to Laugh at the Devil

I remember once when I was so upset over a situation that was happening with a relationship in our church. There was a divisive person who was very influential and charismatic, and this person had decided to spread the division throughout our church body. It was causing my husband and me a lot of pain because this person seemed unstoppable. Relational destruction was following like a whirlwind faster than we could intervene.

I knew that the joy that God had for me surpassed any pain that was nipping at my heels. So, instead of going after the devil's juggler by binding, loosening, cursing, and commanding the problem away in prayer like any good powerful intercessor warrior would, I chose to seek the voice of my bridegroom Jesus. I knew if I could just hear His beautiful voice, it would be far more freeing and powerful than any prayer I could pray out of pain or desperation.

I knew if I could just hear His beautiful voice, it would be far more freeing and powerful than any prayer I could pray out of pain or desperation.

That evening I lay in my bubble bath, soaking in the presence of God with a single candle burning, saying to Jesus, "I don't want to leave here until I hear Your voice. Your voice brings me joy, and if I hear You speak to me, I will be filled with such joy that everything else will melt away. God, please speak to me." Then I waited in silence.

After what seemed like forever but actually was probably about twenty minutes of silence, I had a physical manifestation of His hand. I had been looking up toward the ceiling into the blackness, just staring and hoping for a vision while I waited, when suddenly I felt the hand of God grab my chin and pull it down to where my eyes met the candle that was flickering with one small flame. The minute my eyes looked at the candle, the flame grew about an inch and split into three parts, like three different tongues lapping into the darkness. Then I heard His voice. He said, "Gives a whole new meaning to the Trinity, doesn't it?"

I began to laugh so hard. He had split the flame into three parts, but it was still one flame. What did this trinity flame of God have to do with my problem? It had absolutely nothing to do with what I was going through. It was the voice of my God and the amazing explanation of the Trinity that gave me such joy.

The whole problem I was having with the person trying to divide our church disappeared in an instant. It meant nothing to me. The pain was immediately gone; the problem was so small, and my joy was so big because my God had spoken to me. The joy of the Lord was truly my strength. He wasn't worried about anything. The wayward child was not a threat to Him. Nothing I could have said to the devil would have given me the *chara* joy that Jesus had for me through His amazing voice and revelation of Himself.

So many of my intercessors don't understand why I no longer feel it necessary to get into screaming matches with the devil. It is because the devil does not bring me joy. Screaming at him just makes me madder. I now seek the joy of the Lord through His amazing wisdom and voice in my heart. His joy becomes my weapon of strength, and my ability to laugh with God in the midst of my pain brings incredible release from the scheme of the devil to bind me through fear, pain, and depression.

"Why are the nations in an uproar and the peoples devising a vain thing? The kings of the earth take their stand and the rulers take counsel together against the LORD and against His Anointed, saying, 'Let us tear their fetters apart and cast away their cords from us!' He who sits in the heavens laughs, the Lord scoffs at them." ~Psalm 2:1-4

If the Lord can laugh at His enemies, why can't I? That word laughs means mocks and ridicules. The Lord my God actually mocks and ridicules in His laughter toward the enemies of the Kingdom. Here is the picture I get. The enemy makes his threats toward God's plan on earth, and God grabs His stomach with a huge chuckle followed by the scoffing phrases "whatever," "yeah, right," "ha, ha, ha, that's funny," "ooh, I'm so scared!" "not!" "is that the best you've got?" and "get out of here; you're killing me with your humor!"

His inner strength is my assurance that He's God of the entire universe, so who is this imbecile enemy threatening His will or His people? His calm delight and gladness of heart reflect His knowledge that absolutely no one or nothing will ever conquer Him or His people.

Listening to the voice of God through His laughter in the heavens and on earth is another way to rise up in victory and defeat the enemies that are trying to defeat you through grief and depression.

Listening to the voice of God through His laughter in the heavens and on earth is another way to rise up in victory and defeat the enemies that are trying to defeat you through grief and depression.

"But now I come to You; and these things I speak in the world so that they may have My joy [chara] made full in themselves. I have given them Your word; and the world has hated them, because they

are not of the world, even as I am not of the world." ~*John 17:13-14 (bracketed text mine)*

Jesus prayed this prayer to the Father before He was to be crucified. His goal was to speak His words of life to the world. Through His voice, through His words, He would impart His *chara* joy to those who had ears to hear Him. Not only would He pass on His gladness of heart and calm delight into their lives, but inner strength and assurance would be made full in them.

The will of the Holy Spirit is to make joy dominant in your life, completely separate from your outward circumstances.

Jesus is still available to come to us and speak His very words to our heart so we can be full of His joy. The will of the Holy Spirit is to make joy dominant in your life, completely separate from your outward circumstances. Always remember that the *joy* fruit of the Spirit does not originate from us but from heaven.

Time to Pray

If you have a deficiency of the *joy* fruit of the Spirit in your life and want to be healed, pray this prayer.

"Heavenly Father, I come to You and ask You to make Your chara joy evident in my life in spite of the circumstances that I go through. I trust You in my times of testing and will rely on You to be joyful through me. Give me discernment when I am outside of Your heavenly joy. I want Your joy to be my inner strength and assurance,

and I want Your gladness of heart and calm delight anchoring my actions. I want to laugh with You at the enemies that seek to destroy me through depression and grief. Let me laugh with You now! In Jesus' name, amen."

Time to Apply

After completing Chapter Four in your *Life Enhancement Journal* at the back of the book, turn to Chapter Five: *The PEACE of God Passes Understanding.*

Chapter Five

The PEACE of God Passes Understanding

*W*hen the storms of life rage and the winds blow, *peace* fruit of the Spirit is the most valuable quality of the nature of God to have at hand. Is it possible to have peace deep within when hurricane winds of life are blowing all around us? Yes, the *peace* fruit of the Spirit resides within our souls, a precious gift from God. Jesus, known as the Prince of Peace, shares His peace with us through the Holy Spirit.

"Peace I leave with you; My peace I give to you; not as the world gives do I give to you. Do not let your heart be troubled, nor let it be fearful." ~John 14:27

Jesus said His peace was not the same as the peace the world had to offer. It was instead the kind of peace He was giving us through the Holy Spirit, a peace that would keep our hearts from being "troubled" or "fearful." Jesus compared His peace to what the world could offer and said it was nothing like it.

One kind of peace that the world strives for is displayed on the bumpers of cars and trucks with decals reading "Peace not war" or the peace sign, a circle with a three-pronged claw inside. This peace is understood by the world to mean the absence of external conflict. When the fighting stops, then there will be peace. The peace that Jesus spoke of, in contrast, is an inner peace of the soul. This is the peace that He has. This is the peace given to every believer through the Holy Spirit. It is the *peace* fruit of the Spirit.

The biblical word *peace* comes from the Greek word *eirene,* which means stillness of soul, quietness, rest, set at one again, not torn apart, made whole and complete. When the Bible says, "Peace be with you," it is saying, "May you enter into oneness with God; may you not feel separated or torn apart from who He is; may you not be distracted or restless in your existence; may you be restored back to the whole and complete man or woman that He has made you be; and may you be one in mind, purpose, and mission with God, who loves you and has created you for His good pleasure."

Peace: The Mark of the Kingdom

We know that when Jesus spoke of peace, He was not alluding to the absence of earthly conflict. In Matthew 10:17-42, He spent a lot of time warning His disciples that they would be facing persecution for their faith. He said they were not to question the reasons for it, nor were they to fear the betrayal that was to come as a result of it, even from family members. He supported this warning by explaining that His purpose was not to bring the peace [*eirene*] of the world, or absence of conflict, but radical and dangerous world conflict instigated by faith in Him. He quoted Micah 7:16 in this passage, the words about fathers and daughters even being at war against members of their own households.

"Do not think that I came to bring peace [eirene] on the earth; I did not come to bring peace [eirene], but a sword. For I came to SET A MAN AGAINST HIS FATHER, AND A DAUGHTER AGAINST HER MOTHER, AND A DAUGHTER-IN-LAW AGAINST HER MOTHER-IN-LAW; and A MAN'S ENEMIES WILL BE THE MEMBERS OF HIS HOUSEHOLD." ~Matthew 10:34-36 (bracketed text and emphasis mine)

> *As followers of Jesus Christ, we have the peace fruit from heaven. This peace fruit is evident by the stillness of soul and oneness with God that we have on display in the midst of the conflicts.*

Because of the restlessness and selfishness in the souls of mankind upon the earth, conflict will never cease; but as followers of Jesus Christ, we have the *peace* fruit from heaven. This *peace* fruit is evident by the stillness of soul and oneness with God that we have on display in the midst of the conflicts. Jesus was saying that believers in Him would not be torn apart in their ability to love God and mankind as well. The holders of God's peace within their inner being as *peace* fruit of the Spirit would be able to walk in wholeness of mind, purpose, and mission through any conflict the world had to offer them, even to death for their faith.

The *peace* fruit displayed in your life, especially in times of conflict, will be the evidence of the Kingdom of God present on the earth.

"For the kingdom of God is not eating and drinking, but righteousness and peace [eirene] and joy [chara] in the Holy Spirit. For he

who in this way serves Christ is acceptable to God and approved by men." ~Romans 14:17-18 (bracketed text mine)

The Kingdom of God is *peace* and *joy* in the Holy Spirit. Peace is not merely an *attribute of* the Kingdom or an *attitude of* the Kingdom; it *is* the Kingdom. There is no worry or turmoil in the Kingdom of God. Unrest and fear cannot dwell in the Kingdom, whether it be in heaven, on the earth, or within the believer, where Scripture says the Kingdom of God resides (Romans 14:17).

When Jesus spoke about Kingdom of God in the parable of the vineyard in Matthew 21:23-43, he used the same word for *fruit* that is used for the fruit of the Spirit in Galatians 5:21-23.

"Therefore I say to you, the kingdom of God will be taken away from you and given to a people, producing the fruit [karpos] of it." ~Matthew 21:43 (bracketed text mine)

What is the fruit of the Kingdom? The Greek word for *fruit* here is *karpos*, which is the same word for fruit *[karpos]* of the Spirit *love [agape], joy [chara], peace [eirene], patience, goodness, kindness, faithfulness, gentleness* and *self-control* in Galatians 5:21-23.

In the parable, the vine growers were not harvesting the fruit that the owner had entrusted to them. After they killed two sets of slaves sent from the owner to bring in the harvest, the owner sent his own son. The vine growers then killed the son. The harvest in the vineyard was never realized. The owner was left with the task of making strict judgments upon these thieves and murderers. After bringing the vine growers to their "wretched end," the owner then would rent out the vineyard to vine growers that would "pay him the proceeds at the proper season."

God deserves the proceeds of our lives. The fruit of the Spirit released through us into the world is what He's looking for. The *peace* fruit of the Spirit shows the world that the Kingdom of God is at hand.

Peace: Advances the Kingdom of God

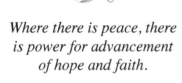

Where there is peace, there is power for advancement of hope and faith.

Because *peace* fruit is the Kingdom of God, in order to advance the Kingdom on the earth, it must be displayed through God's children on earth consistently and in every situation they face. Where there is peace, there is power for advancement of hope and faith. Where there is no *peace* fruit, there is a hope deficiency.

"Now may the God of hope fill you with all joy [chara] and peace [eirene] in believing, so that you will abound in hope by the power of the Holy Spirit." ~Romans 15:13 (bracketed text mine)

This prayer that Paul prayed for the Roman Christians says they would advance forward in hope by the power of the Holy Spirit through the abundant joy and peace given to them by God. For us, it means the *peace* fruit is to be pursued and displayed fervently because where peace abounds, hope and faith will be present with power to move the Kingdom forward, not only in our lives but also our cities. Without peace and joy working together through the Holy

Spirit, we can be swept away by the storms of disarray and chaos. Hopelessness tries to grip our hearts and fear sets in.

Jesus could sleep through the storm while on the journey to the Gaderenes (Luke 8:22-26) because His peace was from another world—heaven, where there are no storms. The *peace* fruit within Him had authority over any storm on the earth. Within Him was the fruit of the Kingdom of God. His oneness with the Father released the Kingdom in Him.

When He was awakened by His disciples, He did not respond favorably to their display of panic, even though they coated their anxiety with their need for Jesus to pray and deliver them. We might think He would have been flattered for their boldness to wake Him and trust Him to "save the day." Instead, the opposite happened. After calming the wind and the seas, Jesus then turned to His disciples and rebuked them for their puny faith. Jesus most likely was enjoying a nap and felt that they should have spoken to the winds and the seas in His Name and let Him sleep.

I can really empathize with Jesus in this story because I hate to be awakened with a crisis, especially, if I don't consider the problem a crisis and there is an easy solution that didn't involve me. It causes me to ask, how many times do we cry out to Jesus in desperation stemming from the lack of *peace* fruit within us being accessed aggressively in our lives?

The peace fruit of the Spirit is divinely ordained to be present in the children of God at all times. It's within easy reach, available right there inside of us through the Holy Spirit.

Some of our crises are perceived merely because of our unawareness of the dormant *peace* fruit that is available in our spirits. The *peace* fruit of the Spirit is divinely ordained to be present in the children of God at all times. It's within easy reach, available right there inside of us through the Holy Spirit. And it needs to be accessed for every situation of conflict and chaos in our lives. We can measure the power the Kingdom of God has in us by the amount of *peace* fruit that we display in our conflicts and chaotic circumstances.

Peace: Extinguishes Fear

Fear is a demonic tool, used by God's enemy the devil, to paralyze God's body the church from reaching energetically for the *peace* fruit. It's time we take hold of the fact that where there is *peace* fruit, there is no fear.

"These things I have spoken to you, so that in Me you may have peace [eirene]. In the world you have tribulation, but take courage; I have overcome the world." ~John 16:33 (bracketed text mine)

Jesus tells the disciples that this world will give them trouble and tribulation. He then proceeds to link the peace that He's giving them to the courage that they can have to overcome the world and all its ungodly influence. It's God's *peace* fruit that will give them the power to dispel the fear that rules the kingdom of darkness. Peace renders fear powerless and thus, another scheme of the devil destroyed! In order for God's Kingdom to dominate the earth and His will to be done and advance on the earth, His followers need to access the *peace* fruit of God. It is available to us 24/7. Aggressively manifesting the peace fruit in our situations is mandatory if we are to overcome, like Jesus did, the world's trials, tribulations, and ungodly systems that are set out by the devil to stumble us.

Peace: Protects the Mind and the Heart

On January 23 in the evening, a good friend of mine received a call from her second child, who was thirty-eight years old. He told her that he had not been feeling well and had gone to the doctor. The doctor had found spots on his liver and had scheduled him for a biopsy. My friend might have gone into panic mode, but all of a sudden, she said, she felt peace like she had never felt before come over her and well up within her. She knew that it was God's peace that was being manifested in her heart and her mind. She immediately went into prayer for her son and felt the perfect peace that God promises.

"Be anxious for nothing, but in everything by prayer and supplication with thanksgiving let your requests be made known to God. And the peace of God, which surpasses all comprehension, will guard your hearts and minds in Christ Jesus." ~Philippians 4:6-8

After this encounter with the Lord, she told me, "I went to work the next day without worry, stress, or anxiety. That morning I spoke with my son's wife and told her about the perfect peace I was feeling concerning what was happening. She was very grateful that I shared this with her."

That evening, my friend received another call, this one from her niece to let her know that her only living sister had collapsed and died that morning. Not knowing whether or not her niece was saved, again she went into prayer to ask God about her salvation. Praying for her and her family was something my friend did often. "Again I experienced the peace that surpasses all human understanding," she told me. "I could feel God guarding my heart and mind. I was assured by Almighty God that He had heard and answered my faithfulness in praying for this family. I was able to go to see my nieces and nephews the following Sunday for a gathering and plant a seed for their salvation."

After the gathering at her sister's home, my friend went the next morning to visit with her son and his family. When she arrived, her daughter-in-law was on the telephone speaking to her son. When she hung up the phone, she told my friend that she had just learned from the doctor that the biopsy of the spots on the liver showed they were benign. "Praise be to God for the peace that He gives us when we most need it," my friend said to me. "I know, I know, what He gave me was an overflow of the peace that surpasses understanding, because I had been in this place before and had not had this level of perfect peace."

What released an abundance of perfect peace in her life when she was facing the potential loss of her son and the loss of her beloved sister? It was the *peace* fruit of the Spirit that was residing within her. Her faith to pray with assurance of God's love allowed God's peace to overflow within her.

The *peace* fruit also protected her heart from coming to God in her own human understanding and doubting turmoil. It guarded her mind so that when she poured out her requests and supplications before God, she was able to have the mind of Christ to pray for His will in both situations. The *peace* fruit also allowed her to pray with authority and receive what heaven wanted to give her for the victory in her circumstance.

Time to Pray

If you have found the need for more of the *peace* fruit of the Spirit in your life, pray this prayer.

"Holy Spirit I need Your peace fruit to be released in my heart, and I go to the Father with my request. I know that He knows what I need before I even ask, but I will still ask because He tells me to bring my needs before Him. Please release the peace fruit of the Spirit of God in me to guard my heart and my mind so I do not ask amiss. Let the peace of God permeate my being so I can enter into that holy place where peace wells up and overflows. In Jesus' name, amen."

Time to Apply

It's time to go to the *Life Enhancement Journal* at the back of the book and turn to Chapter Five. Be sure to pray through the exercise while asking God the questions you may have on peace. When you are finished recording your answers, then proceed to Chapter Six: *Let Your PATIENCE Be Known to Man.*

Chapter Six

Let Your PATICE Be Known to Man

*O*ur God is patient. His mercy endures forever. His patience toward us gives us time to come to Him and become His. If it were not for the patient forbearance of God the Father that keeps Him waiting for mankind to come to Him, He would have destroyed the earth again as He did in the time of Noah because of its great sin. It's His patience that increases the chances for all people on earth to be with God in heaven by the redemptive work of Jesus on the cross.

Patience, long-suffering, perseverance, and *endurance* are interchangeable words found in the Bible that come from the Greek word *makrothymia*, which means forbearance, fortitude, enduring, temperance, and longtime upholding.

The patience *fruit is imperative for the child of God, and it is only fully ripened perfected and manifested in times of great pressure.*

To have patience is to be able to forbear, or hold up without crumbling, under pressure. Patience is continuing with endurance under stress. The *patience* fruit is imperative for

124

the child of God, and it is only fully ripened perfected and manifested in times of great pressure. Fully ripened patience is the result of weathering; its emergence is similar to what happens to clay when it is tempered by fire. The tempering process for clay in fire allows for its perfected use, upholding without cracking or breaking, chipping, or being crushed under the load. Tempered glass is created with the same outcome in mind. It is a glass that won't shatter under pressure or violent blows.

Patience is perfected, long-suffering is learned, and perseverance is accomplished through fire. When you pray for *patience* fruit, it is manifested in you as you go through the fire and undergo the heavy load-bearing process. Having the *patience* fruit is a work of the Holy Spirit in your life as a result of your encountering various and several trials and tribulations. God never gives us more "fire" than we can handle without Him, but always more provision than we would ever ask for from Him. He allows our load to get just heavy enough that it feels like we will break. When He allows our trials to weight us down as far as they can without breaking us, then the blessing of patience comes and our perseverance muscles are built up stronger than before the encounter.

Perfected patience follows the raising of our endurance level. The *patience* fruit of the Holy Spirit is displayed in us more and more as we allow Him to endure the increased pressure for us. When the Holy Spirit endures our pressures for us, He also releases the *joy* fruit in our lives. We are encouraged in Scripture that joy combines with patience through our trials and proves our character when *agape love* fruit is displayed.

"Consider it all joy [chara], my brethren, when you encounter various trials, knowing that the testing of your faith produces endurance. And let endurance have its perfect result, so that you may be perfect and complete, lacking in nothing." ~James 1:2-4

Patience: Produces Hope

Why is it so important that we have an abundance of hope in our lives? Without hope we are like a ship without an anchor. It is hope that anchors our soul and gives us the stability to pursue the *peace* fruit of God in our trials. Without hope there is no peace, and where there is no peace there is no faith. Where there is no faith, there is no pleasing God. Where there is no pleasing God, there is no favor. It is the release of the *patience* fruit in our lives that keeps us building the life and character of God Himself in us. Trials and tribulations are what produce and allow the *patience* fruit to be released to grow the likeness of God in our lives.

> *It is hope that anchors our soul and gives us the stability to pursue the* peace *fruit of God in our trials.*

"Therefore, having been justified by faith, we have peace [eirene] with God through our Lord Jesus Christ, through whom also we have obtained our introduction by faith into this grace in which we stand; and we exult in hope of the glory of God. And not only this, but we also exult in our tribulations, knowing that tribulation brings about perseverance; and perseverance proven character; and proven character, hope; and hope does not disappoint, because the [agape] love

of God has been poured out within our hearts through the Holy Spirit who was given to us." ~Romans 5:1-5 (bracketed text mine)

God's main goal for us on earth is to restore His image back to the world in us. The *patience* fruit of the Spirit *[makrothymia]* is what allows us in tribulation to prove our character, strengthen hope, and lengthen the anchor of stability in our lives. God is the ultimate picture of stability. He does not waiver, He is

The patience *fruit of the Spirit* [makrothymia] *is what allows us in tribulation to prove our character, strengthen hope, and lengthen the anchor of stability in our lives.*

never afraid, and He upholds the world with the Word of His power. He has given us access to His immeasurable *[makrothymia] patience* fruit. What sets us apart from the world, as we know it? The *makrothumia* patience of God that resides within our mortal bodies.

The Goal of PATIENCE: Faith, Preserving the Soul, Receiving The Promise

The Bible speaks about a "need" for patience and confidence in doing the will of God. It speaks about a promise that is to be received as we continue to live by faith, not grow weary and shrink back into destruction when He comes. It is a sobering thought to know that the very promise of our eternal life is directly correlated with our "need" for the *patience* fruit *[makrothymia]* alive and active in our life when He returns.

"Therefore, do not throw away your confidence, which has a great reward. For you have need of endurance (patience) so that when you have done the will of God, you may receive what was promised. For yet in a very little while, he who is coming will come, and will not delay. But My righteous one shall live by faith; and if he shrinks back, My soul has no pleasure in him. But we are not of those who shrink back to destruction, but of those who have faith to the preserving of the soul." ~Hebrews 10:35-39 (emphasis mine)

Paul the apostle is explaining to the Hebrews here that they will be greatly rewarded by God for their confidence and faith in Him at His coming. He says that they are in "need of endurance," which is a definition of patience, so that when they have done the will of God, they may receive what was promised. The promise Paul refers to is eternal life. He goes on to say that in the day of Jesus' return, their soul will have been "preserved." The word *preserving* comes from the Greek word *peripoiēsis,* which is another word for obtaining or keeping. In simpler terms, we "need" the *patience* fruit *[makrothymia],* or the ability to endure the testings in our lives in such a strong measure that in its activation throughout this life, mixed with faith and confidence in God, it will "preserve" or keep the promise of eternal life active in our souls so that when He comes back, we will not have to shrink to destruction but will be able to obtain the promise that we've been living and hoping for on the earth. Do you see how the *patience* fruit of the Spirit in our lives is absolutely crucial to our life on the earth until the day that Jesus returns?

The opposite of *preserve* is to spoil or ruin or lose. We put minerals, such as salt, as well as chemicals in our canned and jarred fruits and vegetables to preserve them so they cannot spoil before we decide to eat them. The process is similar to what happens with the *patience* fruit. The perfected display of patience in our life keeps us from spoiling, ruining, or losing our hope and witness before the great coming of Jesus Christ.

God's first goal of displaying the *patience* fruit of the Spirit in us is faith. His second goal of its display is to preserve our soul for His coming. The third goal of displaying the *patience* fruit of the Spirit is so we will receive His promise of eternal life as we endure to the end. So go after the *patience* fruit with everything within you. Welcome the tribulations and trials in your life because they perfect the *patience* fruit, build faith, and enable you to preserve your soul to receive the promise of eternal life at His coming.

Welcome the tribulations and trials in your life because they perfect the patience *fruit, build faith, and enable you to preserve your soul to receive the promise of eternal life at His coming.*

The Outcome of PATIENCE: Life

I have met many competitive athletes. Marathon runners are my favorite endurance trainers. One runner friend of mine told me that it was the building up of their mental and physical patience (endurance) that allowed them to even finish their race. Marathon runners are a great picture of endurance because the pressure they put themselves under to get in shape for each race is downright excruciating. Rigid dietary plans, persevering through inclement weather patterns, and continuous momentum in spite of body aches and pains are just a few of the disciplines that build their endurance. Jesus talked to his disciples about a similiar training experience and fruitful outcome with respect to the endurance, or patience in faith, that would eventually save their spiritual lives.

"But you will be betrayed even by parents and brothers and relatives and friends, and they will put some of you to death, and you will be hated by all because of My name. Yet not a hair of your head will perish, by your endurance (patience) you will gain your lives." ~Luke 21:16-19 (emphasis mine)

Jesus warns His disciples in this passage of the hardship they would inevitably face for their unshakable faith in Him. Betrayal, misunderstanding, mockery, and even death would be the reactions of the world to them. Even those closest to them—mothers, fathers, sisters, and brothers—would turn on them and hate them because of Jesus. He then goes on to encourage them by saying that their patience would cause them to gain their lives. How would they gain their lives? Through the persecution, the *patience* fruit of the Spirit and the perfect work that it would do in their lives would cause them to last until the end, not wavering in their faith but pressing through with sustaining faith to gain eternal life in the end.

Faith in Him while the going is sweet is good, but the sustaining faith in Him in the flaming heat is the faith that saves us in the end.

Sustaining faith is the means to the outcome. You probably have heard it said that God is not as concerned with our comfort as He is with our character. Likewise, God is not as pleased with our beginning faith as He is with our ending faith. Sustaining faith means sustaining life. Faith in Him while the going is sweet is good, but the sustaining faith in Him in the flaming heat is the faith that saves us in the end.

God is looking to develop a people who are fearless. Faith is the opposite of fear. As the world draws to the end, the warm love *[agape]* of many will become cold, and a delusional spirit will be released upon the world that causes many to fall away (1 Timothy 4:1). If we develop our endurance, our *patience* fruit, our fortitude for the will and knowledge of God now, we will be able to stand firm with all assurance and faith in the end times. In his first letter to Pastor Timothy, the apostle Paul reiterates the importance of developing perseverance to the end. This perseverance would ensure salvation.

"Pay close attention to yourself and to your teaching; persevere [makrothymia] in these things, for as you do this you will ensure salvation both for yourself and for those who hear you." ~1 Timothy 4:16

Each one of us has to undergo trials and tribulation on the earth. I remember a trial in my life that caused me much grief and called me to expend more faith than I had developed in my life up to that point. As I was "running out" of my developed faith, I began to grumble and complain about my circumstances. After about two weeks of finding myself whining and complaining in my prayer time or in my car driving down the road in conversation with God, He spoke these words to me: "Wendi, it is imperative that you are tested right now, so what would you trade instead of this trial I have picked for you?"

I was taken back a bit with the question, and I said, "What do you mean, what would I trade for this trial, Lord?"

He said the same thing again. His words this time were: "It is your turn for a trial to continue the perfecting of your faith. I have chosen this trial for you at the current time, but since you don't like this one, what would you trade for it?"

I began to consider my life more closely. Let's see. My child was healthy and serving the Lord. I was healthy with a good job and a great family. My husband was healthy with a great job. All my animals were healthy. Our friends and extended family were prosperous, alive, and healthy. Gee, would I trade anything in my life for a different trial than the one I was undergoing?

It was at that moment that I began to repent. I realized that my gracious Heavenly Father in His great mercy had handpicked my current trial, and He was there in it with me to use it to perfect endurance and *patience* fruit in me.

You see, *patience* fruit isn't perfected and on display while you are exercising developed faith. Patience is made perfect when you move into areas of your life where faith has not been developed. As you endure and call upon the grace of God when all your developed faith is gone, then you expand and grow larger and stronger faith muscles.

"Consider it all joy, my brethren, when you encounter various trials, knowing that the testing of your faith produces endurance [makrothymia]. And let endurance [makrothymia] have its perfect result, so that you may be perfect and complete, lacking in nothing." ~James 1:2-4 (bracketed text mine)

Here's one last story that will encourage you to continue on, joyfully encountering God in your trials until He comes for you. I had a vision during one of my trials. God speaks to me a lot in visions and dreams, and I believe they are something to ask Him for on a regular basis. His ways are not the ways of the world. The world would say, and unfortunately much of the Christian bride of Christ that still relies on the world's standards would say, that seeking God in visions and dreams is not using faith. I say, hey, if they were good for Paul the apostle, John the beloved, Samuel the prophet, Peter the apostle, David the righteous king, Nebedchennezer the wicked king, and countless others in the Bible, then they are good for me as well.

Here's the vision I had that day. I was riding a ten-speed bicycle down a beautiful, freshly paved, two-lane country road with no yellow dividers on the middle of the road, only fresh black pavement. Zipping right along with the hot sun beating down my back, I was definitely sweating but enjoying the ride tremendously. I had no water bottle with me, so I was feeling a bit dehydrated, but I still had strength for the journey on this long, lonely highway. There was no scenery to speak of, no animals to gaze at, no mountains in the distance. It was just a lonely, long straight highway on a hot summer day with no end in sight and no water to cool me off or quench my thirst.

I wasn't afraid or worried at all. In fact, I knew I would have the strength to make it to my destination even with no water available. I had the faith to know how I could conserve my energy and maintain my strength for this long journey. I was very conscious that God had put me on this road, so I knew that when I needed water, it would be there for me. I also knew that the sun would be going down soon, so the heat of the day would not exhaust me much longer. I had all faith that I would make it to my destination and there would be no problems along the way other than a tiresome journey.

I had been traveling on my bike about fifty miles. I was really thirsty, sweaty, and beginning to experience fatigue beyond my physical ability to go on. All of a sudden, I noticed I was approaching the end of the pavement I had been riding on. Ahead of me I saw very deep, pure white sand. Have you ever tried riding a ten-speed bicycle in deep sand? I was very fatigued, and my muscles were burning with over exhaustion. To peddle any farther would be virtually impossible.

As I came closer to the sand, I began to panic. I knew my bike would not make it even twelve inches in this sand without falling over. My journey was over. I was without water, and I was stranded on this road with no will to go on. I'd never make it to my destination. I began to put my brakes on and stop before my tire reached the sand. My thought was to stop at the end of the pavement, look up to heaven in exhaustion, and wait for the next word from God.

When I began braking and before I hit the sand, the Lord said, "I don't want you to stop at the sand. I want you to increase your speed. I want you to gear up to your highest gear and continue peddling. Prepare to hit the sand, peddling with all the strength that's left within you. I want you to go as far and as fast as you can. If you slow down, Wendi, you'll not go as far as I need you to go. I know that you won't get very far, but if you gear to your lightest gear, you will be able to exert the remaining of your raw faith and energy and gain some ground."

I obeyed the Lord, slamming my gear into speed ten at about twenty feet before the end of the pavement. I hit the sand with a thud, peddling so fast and yet only gaining about an inch at a time. When my bike began to wobble, I used every muscle in my body to stay above the sand. I peddled until the burn in my legs seemed unbearable. Keeping my heart fixed on the words He had spoken to me, I understood then that He would not be carrying me supernaturally to places that I was unable to will myself to peddle. He would continue to give me the ability to peddle as long as I was willing to continue on, gaining ground in the sand in spite of the pain in my legs, torso, heart, and my mind. I had to determine how long I was willing to press through the agony and continue peddling amidst the unbearable loss of hope and the fruitless effort I was displaying.

As soon as I fell over, about ten feet later, God spoke to my heart and said, "Congratulations, my sweet daughter. I will now pave your road another ten feet."

It astonished me that He did not criticize me for the lack of "muscle faith" to go farther than I had but instead rewarded me for the amount of "raw, enduring muscle faith" I had to continue on when I didn't think I could go any farther. He had spoken to me as a proud father, acknowledging that I had given the task all I had in me and beyond what I thought was my ability to persevere. The ground I had gained was all based on my willingness to press on no matter what the pain, the cost, the humiliation, or the defeat ahead of me. It was gained through my willingness to obey His voice and spend myself on Him, spend the last amount of exertion that had been stored in me. He had assured me that *after* the distance I gained in my vision, persevering through the sand of adversity, He would pave and make a smooth road.

You see, God loves people who are willing to spend themselves on something they don't quite understand and yet, all the while, know that He is the Author of the excursion. Every trial we persevere through develops the *patience* fruit in us that will be needed for the next

> *God loves people who are willing to spend themselves on something they don't quite understand and yet, all the while, know that He is the Author of the excursion.*

excursion. Each time we continue to press forward in love and faith through patience and persistence, our path is paved with victory.

To some of you, this story may seem a little strange. But to many of you, I know that the Spirit of God is witnessing in your spirit that you too want to know Him in ways that are far beyond the human standard.

God has a secret to reveal about your current trial. The Bible is full of Scriptures that speak of Yahweh as a God of Truths and Mysteries (Psalm 25:5; 31:5; Job 11:6; Daniel 2:47; Luke 8:10). He will not reveal anything that has not already been revealed in His Word, but if you ask Him to reveal to you truth and the purpose of your endurance test, He will show you.

The mystery is this: God is God of visions and dreams. He is God of love and righteousness. He is God of blessing and persecution. He is God that cares for you beyond your human understanding. He is God that wants you to know His infinite glory. He is God of prophets, apostles, pastors, evangelists, and teachers. He is God that never changes. He is God that requires your participation. He is jealous God. He is God that wants to have you know Him as much as He already knows you. He is all-powerful God. He is God of miracles. He is uncompromising God. He is God that loves you in your sin as much as He loves you in your desire to wear His righteousness. He is nice, He is sweet, He is pure, and He is holy. He requires you to be holy, which means "set apart."

God desires us, His children, to have the same amount of *[makrothymia] patience* fruit as He has for this world. It's God's patience that gives time for all to come to know Him. His *patience* fruit in us will give us the sustaining faith that is required to remain faithful to Him until the end. When I pray for more patience from God, many people shutter because they have linked patience to pain. In many ways this is a true sentiment; it does take a certain degree of pain in our lives to develop the next level of patience. However, because I know God's hands of mercy and love for me handpick each trial that I go through, I can take hold of His hands and look forward to the victories that accompany my journey in developing the *patience* fruit in my life.

Time to Pray

If you would like God to continue to help you through your journey of developing *[makrothymia] patience* fruit of the Spirit in your life and give you a deeper assurance that He is mercifully hand-picking your situations that will make you reflect Him in greater ways on the earth, pray this prayer.

"God, I thank you for Your desire to make me more like You. I recognize that it is imperative that I go through trials in my life to help develop and release the patience fruit of the Spirit in a greater way. Forgive me for the complaining and doubting that I have displayed toward You and Your people when my trials have become too heavy for me to handle. I admit I cannot go through them alone, and I ask You to come in and let me go through them victoriously, all the while building that sustaining faith that will eventually save and move me into my promise of eternal life. I ask for more dreams, visions, and revelation to give me divine understanding of what You are doing through me and in me during my challenging seasons, and I call upon the Holy Spirit to display Your character of patience in me all along the way. In Jesus' name, amen.

If you prayed this prayer and meant it, then you have captured the heart of your Creator, and you will begin having revelations of your own as to His awesome and mighty love and purposes for you. He has been calling you to know Him for so long, not just in religion but in truth. He has gifts and fruit for you. His gifts are mighty with displays of His power, and His fruit is His very character to be manifested in you.

Time to Apply

Take some time right now to get to know your Father in heaven more. Turn to the back of this book to the *Life Enhancement Journal*. Turn on some soft instrumental music. God can use your favorite music to speak to you, though I recommend Christian music. After you turn on the music, get comfortable, wait before God with an open heart, and ask Him this question: "God, teach me about *[makrothymia]* patience and perseverance." Say to Him, "Father, speak to me about developing the *patience* fruit of the Spirit. Father, what else do You want to share with me regarding patience?"

After your time with the Lord, go on to Chapter Seven: *The KINDNESS of God Leads to Repentance*.

Chapter Seven

The KINDNESS of God Leads to Repentance

*D*o you know there are Web sites in cyberspace that promote random acts of kindness? Do a quick search on the word *kindness,* and you'll see what I'm talking about. Even today's cyber world understands that kindness is a good thing and that it should be spread around to others. Consider the following quotable quotes on the *kindness* fruit of the Spirit.

> *"Constant kindness can accomplish much. As the sun makes ice melt, kindness causes misunderstanding, mistrust, and hostility to evaporate." ~Albert Schweitzer*

> *"Treat everyone with politeness, even those who are rude to you–not because they are nice, but because you are." ~Author Unknown*

Being kind to someone is looked upon as an action demonstrating that the receiver is someone highly favored and worthy of kindness.

Kindness is somewhat expected from us in the human race toward others. Do we think God is to be any different? So much is said about God's anger and His desire to judge the sin in the world with death and destruction. Why is He looked upon as eager to destroy the sinner or the place that the sinner dwells? If God made us in His image and we highly value kindness toward one another, then doesn't it make sense that God highly values kindness toward us as well?

"Or do you think lightly of the riches of His kindness and tolerance and patience, not knowing that the kindness of God leads you to repentance?" ~Romans 2:4

> *The* kindness *fruit motivates us to perform acts of benevolence that are useful and good to others.*

The *kindness* fruit of the Spirit comes from the Greek word *chrēstotēs*, which means benignity and integrity. It comes from an inward morality that causes us to be fit for good use, virtuous, mild, pleasant (as opposed to harsh, hard, sharp, bitter), benevolent, and void of bringing harm. The Holy Spirit desires to produce the same character qualities in us as are found in God the Father. The *[chrēstotēs] kindness* fruit is given to us so we can be mild mannered and pleasant as opposed to harsh, hard, sharp, and bitter. The *kindness* fruit motivates us to perform acts of benevolence that are useful and good to others.

God Is Kind

God is kind. Yes, He hates sin, but He loves the sinner. When I am praying for someone to come to know God, my first prayer is, "Lord, do something really nice for this person today." When I am frustrated with people who call themselves Christians and yet are not living lives that are glorifying to God, I first pray for more of God's kindness upon their lives. "Lord, show them more of Your kindness today so they will repent of their wickedness and see how lovely You are.

Praying in this way is one example of how we can love our enemies, as mentioned in the book of Luke.

"But love your enemies, and do good, and lend, expecting nothing in return; and your reward will be great, and you will be sons of the Most High; for He Himself is kind [chrēstos] to ungrateful and evil men." ~Luke 6:35 (bracketed text mine)

Wow. God is kind *[chrēstos]* to ungrateful and evil men. Do you know people who are ungrateful? Ask God how you can be kind to them. Do you know people who are evil? Ask God how you can be kind to them. Be like God, and be more kind!

A Vision

The Lord woke me up one morning at about 2 a.m. and asked me to get up and pray. I went to my living room and put on some soft, instrumental worship music. I like to call it "soaking" music. It's what I use to lay myself before the Lord so He can speak to me.

As I lay there before the Lord, I saw a vision. I was flying with Him in the atmosphere, looking down on the world. I had an aerial view. I saw little dots, which I understood represented people. These dots were black in color. There were millions of them, and they covered the whole earth. Then all of a sudden I saw many of these dots moving away from each other, leaving large gaps. I asked the Lord what this movement meant.

"My people are walking in offenses," He said.

The movement of these dots began to grieve me as I watched the gaps between people get bigger and bigger around the world. I watched as the dots repelled off of one another. The gaps that resulted spread throughout the world. I was troubled, and I asked the Lord, "Why so much repelling and gapping between the dots?"

He spoke to me with brokenness in His voice. "Those dots that move are people being repelled by the offenses of others."

It hurt me to know that God's people were offending one another and being repelled by those offenses. It horrified me to watching the gaps become a chasm of emptiness, separating the relationships and closeness of each dot. It was as if there was no hope for unity because people take offense so easily, and then the offenders themselves get offended at the ones who took offense.

I began to weep, feeling hopeless to change anything. I cried out, "What would You have from me, Lord?"

"I'm looking for those who will pursue their offenders," He said.

"Pursue the offenders?" I replied. "Okay, Lord, help me and teach me how."

This vision in the night impacted me so much that I shared it with my women's group the next week. Each of us agreed to make it our mission to contact one person during the week who we knew we had offended or who had offended us in the past, creating a gap in our relationship. An act of kindness from us, with the strength of Holy Spirit, would bridge those gaps and please the Lord.

The next day I looked up the phone number of a woman who I hadn't talked to for five years. I called, but the number was disconnected. I thought my job was done, but the Holy Spirit told me to "pursue" this relationship until she physically crossed my path again. I had no idea if she even lived in the same town, but I agreed to obey what the Spirit had said to me.

The next thing I did was to look up an old email address to email her and say hi. The email I sent didn't come back to me, so I assumed my job was done. Once again the Lord reminded me that to "pursue" meant to continue on until the Lord had her physically cross my path.

I waited two days and didn't hear back from her, so I went online and checked the cyber white pages. I found another phone number under her name, so I tried it. Bingo! I called and left a message. Again I thought my job was done, but the Lord reminded me a third time to "pursue" her until I reached her or the Lord physically brought her in my path. Two weeks went by, and I tried calling one more time with the new phone number. This time she picked up the phone, and I was able to speak with her for at least thirty minutes. It was a wonderful conversation and an act of kindness on my part, not allowing the gap to continue separating us and grieving God.

The Lord has given us everything we need for life and godliness (2 Peter 1:3). He has given to us the fruit of the Spirit—love, joy, peace, patience, kindness, goodness, gentleness, faithfulness, and self-control (Galatians 5:21-23). These virtues are not only attributes of God Himself, but they are the weapons of our warfare that are for the pulling down of strongholds (2 Corinthians 10:4). In the case of my friend, a stronghold was taken down that day by an act of kindness.

Kindness versus Judgment

A day of judgment is coming on the world. We can read about it in the book of Revelation. It's the judgment against those who reject the Son of God, Jesus. God has made a way for all sinners to be forgiven of sin, and it is through the blood of the Son of God, Jesus. God's kindness *[chrēstotēs]* can lead people to repentance; however, judgment will come on the day of judgment for those who reject the kindness of God.

"Behold then the kindness and severity of God; to those who fell, severity, but to you, God's kindness, if you continue in His kindness; otherwise you also will be cut off." ~Romans 11:22

Here again the Greek word used for *kindness* is *chrēstotēs*. This form of kindness is seen in moral goodness, integrity, and benignity. It is used here in contrast to the Greek word for *severity,* which translates as "roughness and rigor." We read that those who "fell" and did not repent will receive the roughness and rigor of God on the day of judgment. But to those of us who are faithful, God's moral goodness, integrity, and benignity is given if we continue in His moral goodness, integrity, and benignity toward others; otherwise, we also will be cut off.

What is the message that we should hear in this verse? The kindness of God is nothing to be taken lightly. It is the nice side of God, the side to which He desires all would respond. As we

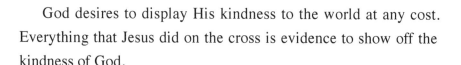

act in the kindness of God toward others, there is no room for judgment, roughness, or rigor.

As we act in the kindness of God toward others, there is no room for judgment, roughness, or rigor.

Surpassing Kindness

God desires to display His kindness to the world at any cost. Everything that Jesus did on the cross is evidence to show off the kindness of God.

"But God being rich in mercy, because of His great love with which He loved us, even when we were dead in our transgressions, made us alive together with Christ (by grace you have been saved), and raised us up with Him, and seated us with Him in the heavenly places in Christ Jesus, so that in the ages to come He might show the surpassing riches of His grace in kindness [chrēstotēs] toward us in Christ Jesus." ~Ephesians 2:4-7 (bracketed text mine)

Everything He did for us while we were in our transgressions and sin He did *so that* He could show us how kind He is. He made us alive with Christ. He raised us up with Him and gave us the authority that His Son has in heaven. He did it all to show us His grace and kindness.

It's important to God that we know and understand His moral goodness, integrity, and benignity. The death of His Son, Jesus, shows us in the most extreme way that everything He does is fit for use, useful, virtuous, good, manageable, mild, pleasant (as opposed to harsh, hard, sharp, bitter), and benevolent. And He gives us the Holy Spirit to live in us so we can display His *kindness* fruit to the world.

God's Intentions Are Kind

What is it about kindness that is so important to God? Wouldn't He get His way faster in people's lives if He were just a little meaner? The Bible tells us in Ephesians that God is motivated by "kind intentions."

"He made known to us the mystery of His will, according to His kind intention which He purposed in Him." ~Ephesians 1:9

We see here that God is full of kind intentions. What is it about being kind that changes people and situations?

Restored by One Thin Dime

During my college years, a shattered relationship left me cold, bitter, and very resentful toward God, the One who loved me more than His own life. I spent about twelve months fighting His gentle whispers at night as my heart ached, even to the point of plotting my own destruction. Jesus appeared to me several times in my pain with His arms outstretched, as if He wanted me to run to Him and allow Him to console me through this time of brokenness. Each time I saw Him or heard His sweet voice, however, I would tell Him to get far from me. How could He allow me so much pain and then want me to run to Him for comfort?

Each new day my hatred for my situation and my life worsened because of my bitter and unbelieving heart. My heart toward God had become jaded and calloused to the point that I didn't care to know what He had to say anymore about things pertaining to my life. The root of bitterness began to defile my path of faith, and I no longer trusted Him to bring anything good to me again.

Finals time came, and one morning I had a ten-page paper due by 8:30 a.m. It was imperative that I got this paper in on time because the instructor was not merciful to those who were late to class. He was known to shut the door and not allow students to enter class if they were as much as one minute late.

Well, I was running late that morning. I arrived at the library at 8:05 a.m. to make copies of my paper. The instructor had demanded not one but two copies of the paper so he could grade one and give it back and keep the other one for future class examples. The copy machine at the library charged 10 cents per copy. I had ten pages to copy and just a dollar to do it, and my class was about a 5-minute walk from the library.

The first dime went in, and the first copy of page one was completed. The second dime went in the machine, and page two was copied. Page three, page four, and then page five were copied. I looked at my watch. It was 8:15 a.m. Page six, page seven, and page eight were copied in good time. The sound of each dime registering on the machine was followed by a smooth release of a page. At 8:20 a.m., page nine came out, smoothly and consistently with all of the others. The humming of the copy machine was like sweet music to my ears. I kept a tight watch on the clock. It was 8:23 a.m.

Page ten. *Chingclunk.* The dime fell through the pay slot and out to the change drop. What? I picked up the dime and reentered it into the pay slot. *Chingclunk.* Not again! What happened? "It's not taking my dime to make my last copy!" I exclaimed to the freshman librarian who was standing by watching me frantically attempt to shake the machine. It was 8:24 a.m.

"Oh God, what's happening? I have to make this last copy or I'm going to be late for class and I will fail this final!" I whispered to myself.

"Change the page in the copier," I heard the Lord say to me in a soft voice. I knew this voice because He had been speaking to me all through my painful time of hardening.

"What do you mean, 'Change the page in the copier?'" I snipped back in a hurry, very irritated.

The same voice spoke very clearly deep in my spirit. "Change the page in the copier to page ten."

When I heard Him say these words to me the second time, I lifted up the copy lid and sure enough, I still had page nine on the glass. God knew I had only enough dimes to make ten copies! I quickly lifted off page nine and replaced it with page ten then put my last dime in the pay slot, and *whalah,* page ten was copied!

At that moment my heart was overflowing with gratefulness toward God that my heart was instantly softened. I began to weep and repent to Him as I ran to my class because His kindness and mercy had been displayed to me in such a great way. My relationship was totally restored to God because of His intimate kindness toward me—with one thin dime. That dime represented the difference for me between an A and an F in my class. I knew I deserved judgment and punishment for the way I had behaved toward Him for the last twelve months in my pain. Instead, because the judgment for my sins had been satisfied at the cross, God displayed an act of kindness, mercy, and grace toward me that changed my life forever.

I had been filled with so much hatred for the one who hurt me and even toward God for letting me go through a broken relationship.

"For we also once were foolish ourselves, disobedient, deceived, enslaved to various lusts and pleasures, spending our life in malice and envy, hateful, hating one another. But when the kindness [chrēstotēs] of God our Savior and His love for mankind appeared, He saved us, not on the basis of deeds which we have done in righteousness, but according to His mercy, by the washing of regeneration and renewing by the Holy Spirit, whom He poured out upon us richly through Jesus Christ our Savior, so that being justified by His grace we would be made heirs according to the hope of eternal life." ~Titus 3:3-7 (bracketed text mine)

The second sentence of this passage says that the kindness of God appeared to mankind. It was the kindness that God displayed to me in the library that melted my heart toward Him that day. In an instant, all the bitterness toward Him was gone. Because I was restored in my love for God, He was then able to heal me of the brokenness I felt from my failed relationship.

Kindness Is a Requirement

God knows what it takes to build a strong and healthy body. As fiber is to the human body, so is kindness a requirement to the spiritual body.

"So, as those who have been chosen of God, holy and beloved, put on a heart of compassion, kindness, humility, gentleness and patience; bearing with one another, and forgiving each other, whoever has a complaint against anyone; just as the Lord forgave you, so also should you." ~Colossians 3:12-13

Because we are chosen by God and belong to Him, He requires from us the display of the kindness *fruit.*

Because we are chosen by God and belong to Him, He requires from us the display of the *kindness* fruit. It is a natural accompaniment to compassion and humility.

Kindness fruit is not necessarily manifested just in what we choose to do but also in how we react to stimulus around us. *Kindness* fruit is reflected in our moral goodness, integrity (truthfulness and honesty), benignity (gracious and harmless), and mild manners (easy going) along with performing acts of usefulness (relevant to the timing and needs of a situation) and virtue (conformity to what is right).

"Be kind to one another, tender-hearted, forgiving each other, just as God in Christ also has forgiven you." ~Ephesians 4:32

God knew that His body of believers on the earth would be made up of so many different personalities, backgrounds, strengths, weaknesses, races, and languages. He knew there would be tendencies between believers to get irritated with one another, forming grudges, resentments, and offenses against one another. In this passage in Ephesians Paul the apostle mentioned the need for kindness to abound in the body.

Kindness fruit preludes a tender heart, which in turns allows forgiveness to flow through the offenses and irritations with one another. In being kind, tenderhearted, and forgiving, we are able to be like Christ, who continually forgives us and shows kindness to us in our times of weakness.

"To sum up, all of you be harmonious, sympathetic, brotherly, kind-hearted, and humble in spirit; not returning evil for evil or insult for insult, but giving a blessing instead; for you were called for the very purpose that you might inherit a blessing." ~1 Peter 3:8-9

Kindheartedness is a portion of the sum of the attributes that we are to portray when dealing with the evil and unlovable, the unruly and the unrepentant. Always give a blessing instead of cursing because a blessing is an act of kindness that originates from the *[chrēstotēs] kindness* fruit that Holy Spirit gives.

Kindness Is Required in Leaders

Leaders face situations every day that challenge the ability to act and react kindly to others. Though there is a place for discipline in the church, everything that is done by leaders in the church should be done with *kindness* fruit. Kindness must not be confused with condoning sin, but *kindness* fruit needs to be present when working with all people, both the righteous and the unrighteous.

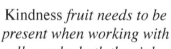

Kindness fruit needs to be present when working with all people, both the righteous and the unrighteous.

"The Lord's bond-servant must not be quarrelsome, but be kind to all, able to teach, patient when wronged, with gentleness correcting those who are in opposition, if perhaps God may grant them repentance leading to the knowledge of the truth, and they may come to their senses and escape from the snare of the devil, having been held captive by him to do his will." ~2 Timothy 2:24-26

There is room for correcting those in opposition to the truth and in need of repentance, but it is to be done with gentleness and *kindness* fruit. God knows what leads people to repentance, and in this Scripture we are told that it's the combination of kindness with gentleness that is needed when correction and discipline are issued. God is the one who grants "repentance leading to the knowledge of the truth." If we stick with His requirement of displaying the *kindness* fruit of the Spirit in all our dealings, then God will be free to minister repentance.

My husband and I once were faced with administering the hardest form of discipline in a church, which is to ask someone not to participate anymore if the guilty one continued to choose rebellion and sin over the righteousness of God. The person was a leader in the church who chose an unholy relationship with another person in the church. Both people had been counseled; they had been prayed over and had gone through various forms of deliverance; and yet one day they both said they were not going to change nor did they want to change.

In that instant, it was evident that my husband and I were to deliver them over to Satan so that their souls would be saved in the last day (1 Corinthians 5:5). It was the hardest thing that we ever had to do because it seemed so harsh, but it was done after much weeping and prayer. It was done as God commanded, with the *kindness* fruit and gentleness. We trusted (and still do so) that repentance will come, as mentioned in 2 Timothy 2:25b.

Time to Pray

If you would like God to fill you with more of the *kindness* fruit of the Spirit, pray this prayer.

"Holy Spirit, I need Your kindness fruit to be released in my heart and my life in a greater way. I now understand that it's Your kindness that leads those who are rebelling against You to repentance. I want to be an agent of kindness so I can release Your convicting power in the lives of the rebellious and reflect Your image to them. I also realize that I need wisdom to be able to be kind when I need to administer discipline to those over whom I have authority. I give You full control, Holy Spirit, to increase kindness fruit in my life. In Jesus' name, amen."

Time to Apply

It's time to go to the *Life Enhancement Journal* at the back of the book and turn to Chapter Seven. Be sure to pray through the exercise while asking God the questions you may have on kindness. When you are finished recording your answers, proceed to Chapter Eight: *Surely GOODNESS and Mercy Will Follow Me*.

Chapter Eight

Surely GOODNESS and Mercy Will Follow Me

*H*ave you ever said, "Oh, for goodness' sake!" or "Goodness, gracious, great balls of fire!" or "Good God Almighty!" as a response to the emotions of anger, surprise, or disgust? These common expressions may seem to be appropriate responses to counteract negative situations, but does the "goodness" in them have any correlation to the *goodness* fruit of the Spirit?

Scripture's word for the *goodness* fruit comes from the Greek word *agathōsynē*, which means valuable, virtuous beneficence, a benefit, or doing well. So the expression "Oh, for goodness' sake," if used in the biblical sense, could be construed to mean "Oh, for the sake of value, virtue, and benefit." The next time you are "spittin' angry," this expression actually would be a "good" (virtuous, valuable, and beneficial) thing to say in light of the many alternatives! It could help spur you on to kindness, which in the flesh is not a normal response to negative circumstances.

Goodness: A Character Quality

The *goodness* fruit of the Spirit is an inner character quality that can manifest itself as a desire to be valuable to mankind through judging fairly and honestly, all the while bringing benefit to others. God's Kingdom is full of goodness, and when we display the *goodness* fruit in our lives, we are bringing the Kingdom of God to earth.

> *God's Kingdom is full of goodness, and when we display the* goodness *fruit in our lives, we are bringing the Kingdom of God to earth.*

Kindness *[chrēstotēs]*, as examined in the previous chapter, means fit for use, useful, virtuous, good, manageable, mild, pleasant (as opposed to harsh, hard, sharp, bitter), and benevolent. The *goodness* fruit *[agathōsynē]* is very similar. The *goodness* fruit and the *kindness* fruit are often sister fruit, meaning they can work together as a family. While *kindness* fruit is at work as the outward expression of what's in the heart, *goodness* fruit is the motivating, inner quality. It is the desire to be valuable and beneficial, often demonstrating truth and honesty. In other words, *goodness* fruit is displayed through mild and pleasant acts that prove to be a benefit to the recipient.

Let's take as an example the woman caught in adultery in John 8:3-11. The religious leaders of the day, the scribes and the Pharisees, catch this woman in the act of adultery, and they bring her to Jesus. They remind Him of the importance of punishing her as the law requires: stoning. Jesus kneels down and begins to write in the dirt. Scripture doesn't say what He's writing, but I believe it's all the different sins that mankind has committed. Then He challenges each one of them to pick up the first stone only if there is one among them who is without any sin.

The *[agathōsynē] goodness* fruit wants truth and fairness displayed in all situations, even if it involves someone having to suffer for it. When Jesus is interacting with the self-righteous mob of religious zealots, the scribes and the Pharisees, He determines that goodness in this situation means applying the principle "what's fair is fair." Jesus says it best when he speaks.

"All right, stone her. But let those who have never sinned throw the first stones!" ~*John 8:7 (NLT)*

Then Jesus displays the *kindness* fruit, which often accompanies the *goodness* fruit, with the next words out of His mouth for her sake.

"Then Jesus stood up again and said to her, 'Where are your accusers? Didn't even one of them condemn you?' 'No, Lord,' she said. And Jesus said, 'Neither do I. Go and sin no more.'" ~*John 8:10-11 (NLT)*

How kind was that? Letting her go, not heaping shame upon her, and surpassing the law of stoning with the law of mercy. But was she off the hook for her sin? No. First, she was released from hypocritical judgment through Jesus' display of goodness and kindness. Next, since goodness means "what's fair is fair" here, Jesus also calls her to repentance. You see, the goodness fruit always wants what's right to triumph over what's wrong. It wants what's fair and true. The path this woman had chosen was not righteous or based in the truth of the God's Kingdom, so Jesus sends her away with the admonition to turn from her sin and do the right thing.

When *goodness* fruit is being displayed in every area of our lives, we not only have mercy toward those who sin, but we have God-ordained exhortation and admonishment on our lips. We can call those in sin to give up the wrong and seek what is right in God's eyes according to Kingdom principles. The *goodness* fruit, when working in conjunction with the *kindness* fruit, results in acts of grace and mercy. In this woman's case, no stoning happened. She was free to go with an admonition from the Son of God to repent.

The Bible speaks of not being easily swayed by darkness but always choosing to walk in the right, or the "light." Here the apostle Paul says that the "fruit of the Light" is goodness, righteousness, and truth.

"For you were formerly darkness, but now you are Light in the Lord; walk as children of Light (for the fruit of the Light consists in all GOODNESS [agathōsynē] and righteousness and truth), trying to learn what is pleasing to the Lord." ~Ephesians 5:8-10 (bracketed text and emphasis mine)

Notice how goodness is listed first here as the fruit of Light. Wherever the Light is, there is *goodness* fruit, righteousness (turning from wrong to right), and truth. Paul is talking to the Ephesian church in this passage, and comparing what the people were like when they were void of the saving knowledge of Christ. He calls this void "darkness" and their new status "light in the Lord." They can know that they are "light in the Lord" by the *goodness* fruit displayed in their lives along with righteousness and truth.

Those of us who are "children of the Light," who have confessed Jesus Christ as our Lord and have dedicated our lives to the purposes of heaven, are under the same mandate as the Ephesians. We are to walk in the Light and learn what pleases the Lord. The good news

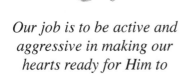

Our job is to be active and aggressive in making our hearts ready for Him to portray who He is to the world through us.

for us about this mandate is that the Holy Spirit lives in us, and the *[agathōsynē] goodness* fruit is from Him. We can let Him reveal what's fair, righteous, and true through us to those who are in need of His goodness, mercy, and salvation. That's His job on the earth! Our job is to be active and aggressive in making our hearts ready for Him to portray who He is to the world through us.

Goodness Releases Works of Faith with Power

I've been committed to Jesus Christ and the purposes of heaven since 1978 and pastoring with my husband in Spirit-filled churches since 1986. I have seen my share of miracles, and yet I still hunger to minister with the kind of power and miracles that Jesus ministered with while He was on the earth. He says in John 14:12 that His disciples will do greater works than He did if they believe. We are his twenty-first-century disciples, so that word is true for all of us.

Sometimes I wonder if the lack of power and authority that we are to have as His disciples is because the *goodness* fruit is not being displayed as God intended through us. Do we really look for ways to do and be good? Do we really rejoice in the

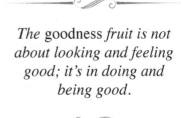

The goodness *fruit is not about looking and feeling* good; *it's in doing and being good.*

truth, or do we turn a blind eye to the evil that is around us without trying to bring loving and gentle correction? I know we like to look and feel good, but *The goodness fruit is not about looking and feeling good; it's in doing and being good.*

The apostle Paul prayed for the Thessalonians to be "worthy" of their calling through their display of goodness and faith with power.

"To this end also we pray for you always, that our God will count you worthy of your calling, and fulfill every desire for goodness [agath-ōsynē] and the work of faith with power, so that the name of our Lord Jesus will be glorified in you, and you in Him, according to the grace of our God and the Lord Jesus Christ." ~2 Thessalonians 1:11-12 (bracketed text mine)

The goal "to this end," says Paul, is to walk in what is pleasing to the Lord: "goodness and the work of faith with power." We see here that displaying goodness and the work of faith with power is very pleasing to God, who is always honest, always fair, always desiring to bring benefit to others, knowing that no one can ever repay Him in the same way He blesses us. His desire is that we have the same desire and virtue within us to express His goodness to the world. Goodness and works of faith with power are mentioned here together as if one ignites the working of the other. The end result is the name of the Lord Jesus being glorified in us!

Goodness on Display

The *goodness* fruit can be in operation inside and outside the four walls of the church building; however, I've seen the greatest display of God's goodness and faith with power released when Christians take Him to those who need salvation and are outside of the church.

I was in Riverside, California, with the Rodney Howard Brown witnessing team in 2009. As we were in the Riverside bus station talking with people, I noticed a Mexican man waiting for his bus. I went up to him and opened the conversation by saying, "Hi, do you know God loves you and has an amazing plan for your life?" He looked at me, smiled, and said, "No," with a little giggle. I proceeded to ask him, "If you were to die in the next two seconds, do you know, without a shadow of doubt, that you would go to heaven?" He said that he did not know. I continued to share the Scripture with him, and he ended up asking Jesus into his heart. It was marvelous. The *goodness* and *kindness* fruit on display released God's power to bring this man to salvation.

Shortly after that conversation, a team member began ministering to a woman in a wheelchair. He prayed the prayer of faith with her, and she got up and began walking and praising God out loud right there in the bus station. She was crying for joy and said that she hadn't been able to walk like that for so long. The Mexican man that had just given his life to Jesus witnessed the whole thing and commented in his broken English, "Wow, is that the power of God?" It was so precious.

The act of going to the bus station and sharing the gospel with others required the *goodness* fruit to be in operation. The desire for honesty was displayed by sharing the truth of the gospel with the Mexican man and the woman in the wheelchair. Wanting to see wrong and injustice corrected was evident there as well. The injustice was that the lady was confined to a wheelchair when our convictions were telling us that Jesus could intervene and make her well. It

160

wouldn't have been fair or honest not to tell her, so we prayed the prayer of faith, and God healed her! Great benefit was brought to all those around. The woman walked, the man witnessed the power of God, and the ministry team there that day benefitted by being able to grow even more in our faith. Everyone gained from the *goodness* fruit in action that day.

When we step out of our comfort zones and let the *goodness* fruit manifest in our lives to bring benefit and value to those who are unable to find it in their own efforts, God releases His power. His love and His goodness are made visible.

When we step out of our comfort zones and let the goodness fruit manifest in our lives to bring benefit and value to those who are unable to find it in their own efforts, God releases His power. His love and His goodness are made visible.

The streets of our cities and towns are full of hungry and cold people who need to eat, find warmth, and hear that God loves them and has an amazing plan for their life. The hospitals are full of the hurting and dying who need someone to ask them the question, "If you were to die today, do you know beyond a shadow of doubt that you'd go to heaven?" The prisons are full to capacity with the forsaken and lonely who need someone to assure them that God has a desire to know them and be known by them. The insane asylums are full of the confused and disoriented who need to know that Jesus sets the captive free and can give them a sound mind. The boys and girls homes are full of the unloved and mistreated who need to know they have a Father in

The lists of opportunities on this earth to let the goodness fruit be released in us and display God's works of power are endless.

heaven who sent His only Son to show them how much He loves them. The lists of opportunities on this earth to let the *goodness* fruit be released in us and display God's works of power are endless.

Goodness to Admonish One Another

At times throughout life we find ourselves in positions of authority. We encounter people we have authority over who need correction, exhortation, and admonishing—in our jobs, our family, and even in the church. It is important that correction, exhortation, and admonishing come from a heart motivated by the *[agathōsynē] goodness* fruit. The apostle Paul speaks to the Romans regarding this issue.

"And concerning you, my brethren, I myself also am convinced that you yourselves are full of goodness, filled with all knowledge and able also to admonish one another." ~Romans 15:14

Being full of goodness and knowledge is the prerequisite to be able to admonish, or correct and encourage one another. Why goodness? Why not the other eight fruit of the Spirit mentioned in Galatians 5:21-23: *love, joy, peace, patience, kindness, gentleness, faithfulness, and self-control?* The reason that Paul commends the Roman Christians for being full of the *goodness* fruit and able to admonish others is because it's easier to take correction from someone who walks in fairness, honesty, and truth and also wants to bring benefit to others. To admonish, exhort, and

> *Being full of goodness and knowledge is the prerequisite to be able to admonish, or correct and encourage one another.*

correct without a heart filled with the *goodness* fruit of the Spirit could cause the message to be ineffective and sometimes even bring emotional and spiritual damage to the one being corrected.

Admonishing someone without your *goodness* fruit displayed, with kindness and through honesty, integrity, and virtue present in a spirit of fairness based upon righteousness in your own life, could set you up for being seen as hypocritical. Hypocrisy is behavior that is rooted in play-acting. It's manifested in playing a part that isn't true to reality. So when your life doesn't display the *goodness* fruit, which by definition is displaying a life of fairness and integrity, then it is hypocritical to bring correction to others for their lack of the same virtue. Children know this better than anyone. If parents say they love God but live like the devil in their dealings, they lose credibility when trying to correct their children for their rebellion and ungodly acts. The *goodness* fruit enables those in authority to live what they preach and bring transformation to those that they admonish, exhort, and correct.

Goodness to Overcome Evil

We all go through trials and suffering in this world, just as Jesus told the disciples they would in John 16:33. Jesus spoke to the disciples about suffering because He wanted to make it clear that suffering is inevitable in the world. Later, during his ministry years, the apostle Peter spoke about the difference between suffering for doing good and the suffering brought on by one's own evil deeds.

163

"For what credit is there if, when you sin and are harshly treated, you endure it with patience? But if when you do what is right and suffer for it you patiently endure it, this finds favor with God." ~1 Peter 2:20

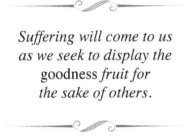

Suffering will come to us as we seek to display the goodness fruit for the sake of others.

Suffering will come to us as we seek to display the *goodness* fruit for the sake of others. Peter says when we patiently endure suffering from doing good, then we find favor with God. On the other hand, no credit is given to us when we suffer for our own sin. In fact, he says that harsh treatment is what we can expect to follow our own sinning.

The apostle Paul speaks to the church in Rome about how God awards the use of the *goodness* fruit with glory, honor, and peace. These three blessings of heaven are given by God to those who choose using the *goodness* fruit over doing evil to all, regardless of race (in this case, Jew or Greek).

"There will be tribulation and distress for every soul of man who does evil, of the Jew first and also of the Greek, but glory and honor and peace to everyone who does good, to the Jew first and also to the Greek." ~Romans 2:9-10

When you find yourself experiencing much tribulation and distress in your home, job, relationships, church, or school, it is a good idea to take an inventory of the level of the *goodness* fruit in your life. Are you suffering for being honest, righteous, and fair? Don't laugh! People suffer every day for standing up for what's right and true. The pro-life movement is a good example. Standing up for the rights of the unborn can mean getting thrown into jail. What about refusing to sleep with your boss for the next big promotion? What about having to pay more taxes because you choose not to lie and cheat on your tax return? How about being willing to lose a friendship because you refuse to turn a blind eye to the domestic violence happening to your friend by turning her husband in and watching him serve time in prison?

When you find yourself experiencing much tribulation and distress in your home, job, relationships, church, or school, it is a good idea to take an inventory of the level of the goodness fruit in your life.

Perhaps you are suffering right now in one of these ways or another because the *goodness* fruit just won't let you compromise your moral standards. If so, the Bible says your reward will be glory, honor, and peace.

Little Goody Two-Shoes

The *goodness* fruit can get a person into a lot of trouble with the ungodly, as is seen in the eighteenth century book, the *History of Little Goody Two-Shoes*. In that tale, a young girl who is very poor but is always the picture of optimism and goodness has only one shoe. When she is given a pair of shoes to wear, she announces to all of her friends that *she* now has two shoes. Those who hear her are jealous and mock her. They are unwilling to accept that the goodness in her brought about the blessing of shoes.

Take a note from *Little Goody Two-Shoes*. Being good and receiving blessings does not always bring popularity. Even in this cute tale, we see that the *goodness* fruit is foreign to worldly standards of behavior. Jealousy and conviction can be stirred in the hearts of those who see God's blessings on those who are good but are lacking the same goodness in their hearts. If your tribulation or suffering is coming from your *goodness* fruit working in full force in your life, then you can rejoice. Jesus calls you extremely blessed!

"Blessed are those who have been persecuted for the sake of righteousness, for theirs is the kingdom of heaven." ~Matthew 5:10

Unfortunately the opposite of "blessed" is true as well. If you are suffering because of a lack of honesty, integrity, or righteousness in your life, then there is no blessing for you. The blessing comes only when you repent, turn back toward God, and are persecuted for the sake of righteousness.

> *God desires every one of us to perfect and display the goodness fruit in our lives.*

God desires every one of us to perfect and display the *goodness* fruit in our lives. Goodness lives within us and originates from God through the workings of the fruit of the Holy Spirit. Aggressively go after it, take hold of its power, and release it in your life. Call upon Holy Spirit to activate more *goodness* fruit in your life.

Time to Pray

If you would like God to release more of the *goodness* fruit of the Spirit, please pray this prayer.

"Holy Spirit, I need Your goodness fruit to be released in my heart and my life in a greater way. I now understand that it's Your goodness operating in my heart that will allow me to release more power into my life and the life of others. I want to be an agent of honesty, integrity, and virtue. I want to be like Jesus and go around and do good, bringing benefit to others, so that others will know You. I understand that I need a greater measure of goodness in my life so when I'm called upon to admonish others, I can do it with honesty, sincerity, and righteousness before You and give them opportunity to be changed and transformed without hypocrisy. Give me grace to suffer for the goodness fruit in my life; and if I am suffering for the lack of goodness in my life, I repent and ask You to forgive me for my sins. In Jesus' name, amen."

Time to Apply

It's time to go to the *Life Enhancement Journal* at the back of the book and turn to Chapter Eight. Be sure to pray through the exercise while asking God the questions you may have on the *goodness* fruit. When you are finished recording your answers, then proceed to Chapter Nine: *Your FAITHFULNESS Reaches to the Sky.*

Chapter Nine

Your FAITHFULNESS Reaches to the Sky

*H*ave you noticed lately that media and restaurants are doing their best to condition us to eat the lighter foods—low fat, low sugars, low sodium, low calories? Thin and light has always been in and right! Right?

I've often asked myself, "Wendi, why do you always have to be so heavy and intense?" When I was younger (in my teens before I gave my life to Jesus), I thought something was wrong with me because I took everything the important people in my life said to me as a "weighty matter." Their statements to me were worth trusting, I reasoned; and I had an innate responsibility to be true to my friends, family, and those I committed my heart to in relationships. I chose to believe everything they told me. I had no reason to doubt them and their sentiment for me.

On the other hand, I was able to look beyond the facade and surface of others not close to me in relationship and see deeper into their hearts. I couldn't understand, for example, why someone would promise to do one thing and then in the next breath, breach that promise or at best compromise what was said. I often wondered where the disconnect was from the individual's mouth to the heart and then ultimately to the feet. Was it in the distance from the mouth to the heart or the heart to the foot? Scripture says that out of the heart the mouth speaks, but once the mouth speaks, the feet can act in ways quite to the contrary.

For these people, I was stunned at the smallest things that would trip up a promise. They would say they'd meet me at 2 p.m. and then not show up till 2:30 p.m. or sometimes not at all. Sometimes, but not often, I'd get a call a half hour or so later to say the time no longer "worked" for them. More typically, it was no call, no show. When I was of dating age, I became familiar with those "I'll love you forever" statements. Two weeks later, the guy would find someone else.

The world is filled with broken promises, failed friendships, and shattered marriage vows; tainted job performances, breached contracts, and unfulfilled goals (usually due to unwillingness to take the step to realize them). What's wrong with this picture?

The *Faithfulness* Fruit of the Spirit

The lack of the *faithfulness* fruit of the Spirit is the root of distrust, disheartening, and disappointment. The Greek word *pistis* for our word *faithfulness* is defined as loyal, worthy of trust, reliable, proof, pledge, confidence, and fidelity.

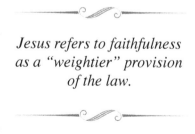

Jesus refers to faithfulness as a "weightier" provision of the law.

The Bible has a lot to say about the faithfulness of God and of mankind. Jesus refers to faithfulness as a "weightier" provision of the law.

"Woe to you, scribes and Pharisees, hypocrites! For you tithe mint and dill and cumin, and have neglected the weightier provisions of the law: justice and mercy and [pistis] faithfulness; but these are the things you should have done without neglecting the others."
~Matthew 23:23 (bracketed text mine)

In other words, faithfulness in God's eyes is not something to be handled lightly. The easier things to give as an offering to God are mint, dill, and cumin, those herbs that grow easily and quickly and take little sacrifice to give away. You also can give of yourself if it's easy and doesn't require a sacrifice. But what really matters to God is what you do when your commitments, those things that may cost you something and affect you in a greater measure, get tougher to follow through on.

The commitments that take something away from us that is difficult to replace, such as valued time, money, and emotions, draw from us a greater need for selflessness. In these commitments is where the *[pistis] faithfulness* fruit is tested in our lives. They are the "weightier provisions" we tend to enjoy and hold onto: the popcorn with the butter, the cola with the sugar, the pretzels with the salt, the milk with the fat.

When Jesus spoke about the "weightier provisions of the law" being justice, mercy, and faithfulness, He was saying that these attributes in obedience of His ways are what get God's attention.

They are the real deal, not the "lite" version, the artificial replica, or what's easier on us to sacrifice.

When Jesus spoke about the "weightier provisions of the law" being justice, mercy, and faithfulness, He was saying that these attributes in obedience of His ways are what get God's attention. "Weightier" in the words of Jesus actually means heavy, with more credibility. "Justice" is a judicial word that speaks of right decisions and right judgment. "Mercy" speaks of compassion. "Faithfulness" speaks of reliability, confidence, and worthiness of trust. Jesus refers to the true law keeper as one who is worthy to be trusted, compassionate, and makes right decisions, not just one who gives away something that comes easily. He also says not to forsake the lighter provision but just include it with the "weightier provisions" of justice, mercy, and faithfulness.

I often have asked myself as a pastor, when hiring a person for a position of ministry or enlisting a volunteer to help move the mission of the Kingdom forward on the earth, what the most important attribute or character quality the person must have. Would I prefer someone who's faithful, who's always there, who does what he or she says, and is someone I can rely on and put my confidence in to perform the tasks given? What if the person struggles to display one or more of the godly character qualities such as love, joy, peace, patience, kindness, goodness, gentleness, and self-control? Would I prefer someone who displays the *love* fruit and yet lacks the *[pistis] faithfulness* fruit? Someone who is kind with others but can't be trusted? Someone who is great at being gentle in harsh situations but doesn't show up when expected?

This question has been difficult for me to answer, but I have found that if I can rely on someone and put my confidence in that person, I can disciple him or her in the development of the other godly character qualities. Someone who is faithful to show up and is trustworthy is someone who can learn to love better and be more patient with team members.

If we look at the chain links of God's character, we see that *faithfulness* is listed near the end of the fruit chain. *Love* is the first in the chain because it is a great summary of who God is, the summation of the other fruit to follow, and is the greatest new commandment of how to be Jesus' friend. *Faithfulness* is listed as fruit number seven in the chain, just before *gentleness* and *self-control*, the last beads to be strung before the clasp is added to hold the necklace or bracelet on securely. I see faithfulness as that often neglected but crucial piece of the chain that reinforces the chain of God's character. A lack of the *[pistis] faithfulness* fruit can bring to naught the other eight character traits of God in one's life.

A good example of this is in our church we periodically look for volunteers to work with our children. We pray and ask the Lord for gifted people who are loving, peaceable, and gentle in dealing with young souls. After a successful campaign of "roping" in new volunteer, gifted teachers who pass the rigorous application process and background checks, we make out our schedule for the quarter. Believe it or not, in a bunch of ten new teachers will be at least two teachers that can't be counted on. The no-call-no-shows or the calling-in-sick-at-the-last-minute routines completely nullify any gifts, talents, or even other fruit they may display toward the kids. Their lack of *[pistis] faithfulness* fruit disqualifies them from working on our team.

The word of God created everything that is seen and unseen. The faithfulness of God to do what He says is what actually holds the world together (Hebrews 1:3). It's the faithfulness of God that gives us hope to believe we will receive the promise of eternal life through faith in His Son Jesus. When the day is done, all nine of the fruit of the Spirit are crucial to advancing the Kingdom, but I have found that without the fruit of the Spirit *faithfulness* in a person's life, it's difficult for that person to be trusted with responsibility.

When faithfulness is missing, the mission can be compromised or destroyed. Unfaithfulness in a marriage, for example, can lead to dissolution of the marriage. When unfaithfulness is present in job performance, it can lead to dissolution of the job. In other words, good things can end when there is a lack of the *[pistis] faithfulness* fruit of the Spirit.

In the movie *Jerry Maguire* with Tom Cruise is a scene where he comes back to his wife and tries to convince her to take him back. She is sitting in a room full of women gathered for a women's support group. He walks into the group and begins to tell her how important she is and what a jerk he's been. She stops him in the middle of his speech and says to him, "You had me at hello." It's the same with faithfulness. You can win people with faithfulness or lose them through lack of faithfulness.

I married my husband, Eric, because he was so faithful to keep our friendship going. Our marriage has lasted since June 28, 1986, because of his faithfulness to me, my faithfulness to him, and our faithfulness to serve our God and live out our destinies together. We started our church on December 28, 2003, and now are in our twelfth year of pastoring in the Reno/Tahoe area, and I believe the ministry remains strong because of our faithfulness to persevere through the good times and the hard times and because of people's faithfulness to pray, partner with the mission, and receive our mentorship and spiritual guidance in their lives.

God Is Faithful and True

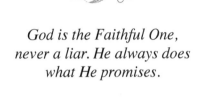

God is the Faithful One, never a liar. He always does what He promises.

God is the Faithful One, never a liar. He always does what He promises. He is trustworthy, He can be relied upon, and He is the only who is worthy of our total confidence. The Bible is very clear that if there is ever any discrepancy in what's been said versus what's been done, it's because man is the liar, not God.

"What then? If some did not believe, their unbelief will not nullify the [pistis] faithfulness of God, will it? May it never be! Rather, let God be found true, though every man be found a liar, as it is written, "THAT YOU MAY BE JUSTIFIED IN YOUR WORDS, AND PREVAIL WHEN YOU ARE JUDGED."" ~Romans 3:3-4 (bracketed text and emphasis mine)

Our lack of faith in God will never move Him to become unfaithful. It's impossible for Him to do two things: to lie and to be unfaithful.

"Whoever receives His testimony has set his seal of approval to this: God is true. [That man has definitely certified, acknowledged, declared once and for all, and is himself assured that it is divine truth that God cannot lie]." ~John 3:33 (AMP)

God cannot lie. There is nothing in His nature that can deceive or trick. Every word that comes out of His mouth is truth, absolute and eternal. It's the same with His faithfulness. His reliability is sure. In fact, His faithfulness is wherever He is.

"O LORD God of hosts, who is like You, O mighty LORD? Your faithfulness also surrounds You." ~Psalm 89:8

Faithfulness surrounds God. His work is done in faithfulness (Psalm 33:4). His faithfulness is ever reaching to the sky (Psalm 36:5). His faithfulness destroys our enemies and protects us from evil (Psalm 54:5; 91:4). His faithfulness is to be declared at the end of every day (Psalm 92:2). His faithfulness is for all the generations (Psalm 100:5). He, Christ, is the faithful and true witness of the beginning of creation (Revelation 3:14).

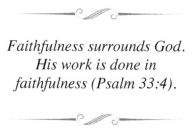

Faithfulness surrounds God. His work is done in faithfulness (Psalm 33:4).

Apostle Paul said it best regarding the faithfulness that dwells in God, that which prevents Him from ever being unfaithful or unworthy of trust.

"For this reason I endure all things for the sake of those who are chosen, so that they also may obtain the salvation which is in Christ Jesus and with it eternal glory. It is a trustworthy statement: For if we died with Him, we will also live with Him; If we endure, we will also reign with Him; if we deny Him, He also will deny us; if we are faithless, He remains faithful, for He cannot deny Himself." ~2 Timothy 2:10-13

Faithfulness Brings Blessing

A blessing is attached to our hardships if we remain faithful to God, to one another, and to our callings and commitments.

I have found in my life that my *[pistis] faithfulness* fruit is tested most when I'm experiencing hardship in my life. Hardships come in many sizes, colors, and flavors. They are different and uniquely fashioned by God for the purpose of enabling us to grow in our faith and in the *faithfulness* fruit of the Spirit. A blessing is attached to our hardships if we remain faithful to God, to one another, and to our callings and commitments.

"If you are reviled for the name of Christ, you are blessed, because the Spirit of glory and of God rests on you. Make sure that none of you suffers as a murderer, or thief, or evildoer, or a troublesome meddler; but if anyone suffers as a Christian, he is not to be ashamed, but is to glorify God in this name. For it is time for judgment to begin with the household of God; and if it begins with us first, what will be the outcome for those who do not obey the gospel of God? AND IF IT IS WITH DIFFICULTY THAT THE RIGHTEOUS IS SAVED, WHAT WILL BECOME OF THE GODLESS MAN AND THE SINNER? Therefore, those also who suffer according to the will of God shall entrust their souls to a faithful Creator in doing what is right." ~1 Peter 4:14-19 (emphasis mine)

In this passage, we see that hardship comes into our lives for the sake of our faith in Christ. Maybe you are ridiculed at your workplace for having or expressing your faith and convictions. Have you ever been asked to lie or cover up an injustice? Perhaps you've had to say no to participating in certain ungodly activities when you are with a group of people that have no fear of God in their worldview. Standing for righteousness, being faithful to your convictions of the truth, can bring hardship upon you. This hardship is what is meant when Scripture says we suffer for the sake of righteousness. The blessing in this hardship is when it is for the sake of God and His purposes, not when it comes from unfaithfulness for the sake of self-ishness or the fear of man.

If you are a murderer, then you are unfaithful to protect and value life. If you are a thief, then you are unfaithful to respect someone else's possession. If you are an evildoer, then you are unfaithful in the opportunities to do the right thing in life situations. If you are a troublesome meddler, then you are unfaithful in protecting and preserving healthy relationships. So when you suffer for being unfaithful in these situations, there is no blessing and sometimes no help from God without repentance. In contrast, when you suffer a hardship because you are faithful to the Creator and act in ways that are faithful to His ways, then you can trust your soul to His *[pistis]* faithfulness to bring you through the suffering victoriously, even if it ends in death, as is true in some cases such as martyrdom.

God Is Faithful in His Promises

There are two types of promises that come from God. Because He is always faithful, we can put our trust in Him to bring them to pass.

The first type of promises we receive from God are *logos* prom-ises. These are all the promises that God makes to us in the written Word of God, the Holy Bible. It's been said by many different scholars that the Bible contains over 3,500 promises. That's a lot of promises. I can't remember any one person in my life making more than five promises to me at one time (some of which I have yet to see fulfilled). So it is difficult for me to grasp God making over 3,500 promises to me! *Logos* promises include Romans 10:9, "If you confess with your mouth Jesus as Lord, and believe in your heart that God raised Him from the dead, you will be saved" and John 14:14, "If you ask Me anything in My name, I will do it." These are written promises in the Word of God.

The second type of promises God makes in the Bible are the *rhema* promises, which are given to us personally as we develop our relationship with Him. The *rhema* promises, also known as revelation promises, never oppose the *logos* promises because He will never contradict His written Word. *Rhema* promises are like "I will give you that special job you've been asking for" and "I will send you to Antarctica." They're revelatory to you, and you receive them when you talk to Him and He talks to you.

> *The word* promise *is used 139 times in the Bible. God loves to make promises, and He loves to keep His promises.*

The word *promise* is used 139 times in the Bible. God loves to make promises, and He loves to keep His promises. His promises are always a resounding YES!

"But as God is faithful, our word to you is not yes and no. For the Son of God, Christ Jesus, who was preached among you by us—by me and Silvanus and Timothy—was not yes and no, but is yes in Him. For as many as are the promises of God, in Him they are yes; therefore

also through Him is our Amen to the glory of God through us." ~2 Corinthians 1:18-20

Knowing that God has over 3,500 promises in His Word, I have decided to be more diligent with my life in finding out what they are. Promises are like a covenant, and they are based on relationship and mutual agreement. If God has a promise for me in His Word but I don't know what it is, is He still obligated to bring it to pass in my life? Although He is faithful to keep them for me, they are activated as I respond in faith to Him.

The most important promise God makes in His Word is the promise of eternal life. It is to those who know Him and serve Him that eternal life is given.

> *The most important promise God makes in His Word is the promise of eternal life. It is to those who know Him and serve Him that eternal life is given.*

"This is the promise which He Himself made to us: eternal life." ~1 John 2:25

Eternal life is one of those promises that is activated in relationship and sustained in a covenant and mutual agreement. Like a marriage. We are the bride of Christ. Our bride status is activated when we "marry" Him through our faith in Him. Until that marriage happens, the promise to live eternally with Him is unable to be activated.

The promise that He made not to destroy the earth with water again affects us whether we believe Him or not because that promise was not made to us personally but as a sign of a covenant between God and the earth itself. This is another example of a *logos* promise.

"I set My bow in the cloud, and it shall be for a sign of a covenant between Me and the earth." ~Genesis 9:13

Noah was present with God when this promise was made and was told to go forth and multiply the earth again. The rainbow was the sign of the covenant to the earth that a flood of that magnitude would never be used to destroy the earth and every living thing again. The rainbow is a visual sign that God is faithful to bring all His promises to pass.

Notice the apostle Paul's faith in God's promises, which he shares in a blessing statement to the Thessalonians.

"Now may the God of peace Himself sanctify you entirely; and may your spirit and soul and body be preserved complete, without blame at the coming of our Lord Jesus Christ. Faithful is He who calls you, and He also will BRING IT TO PASS." ~1 Thessalonians 5:23-24 (emphasis mine)

Faithfulness with Promises, Vows, Oaths, and Commitments

The promises, vows, and relational commitments we make to God and people are not to be made lightly. Being faithful to our spoken and unspoken commitments are of utmost importance to God and those they affect. When unfaithfulness enters in and vows, promises, and commitments are broken or breached, the results can be devastating. Jesus felt so strongly about this truth that He said He preferred

Being faithful to our spoken and unspoken commitments are of utmost importance to God and those they affect.

that these declarations be kept to a minimum and sometimes elimi-
nated all together.

*"Again, you have heard that the ancients were told, 'YOU SHALL
NOT MAKE FALSE VOWS, BUT SHALL FULFILL YOUR VOWS TO
THE LORD.' But I say to you, make no oath at all, either by heaven,
for it is the throne of God, or by the earth, for it is the footstool of
His feet, or by Jerusalem, for it is THE CITY OF THE GREAT KING.
Nor shall you make an oath by your head, for you cannot make one
hair white or black. But let your statement be, 'Yes, yes' or 'No, no';
anything beyond these is of evil." ~Matthew 5:33-37 (emphasis mine)*

Oaths are usually given with some collateral behind them. Phrases
such as "I swear on my mother's grave" and "I swear to God" and
"If I'm lying, may the birds come and pluck my eyes out" are examples of oaths with collateral. "I swear to tell the truth, the whole truth,
and nothing but the truth, so help me God" (with a hand on the Bible
while taking an oath in a courtroom) is another example.

The point Jesus was making in
Matthew 5:33-35 is we shouldn't
make any oaths because many times
we do not have control over those
things used as collateral. We have no
power to control the outcome of the
things that come out of our mouths
by invoking heaven or God as collat-

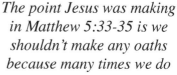

*The point Jesus was making
in Matthew 5:33-35 is we
shouldn't make any oaths
because many times we do
not have control over those
things used as collateral.*

eral. We have no way of assuring that we can be faithful to the oaths
we make. The consequence of breaking an oath is more detrimental
than the need to make the oath to give a commitment to perform.

God can make an oath because God has the power to make it happen and He is infallible in His faithfulness, so there is no chance that He would ever break it. God's promise to Abraham was an oath.

"For when God made the promise to Abraham, since He could swear by no one greater, He swore by Himself, saying, 'I will surely bless you and I will surely multiply you.' And so, having patiently waited, he obtained the promise. For men swear by one greater than themselves, and with them an oath given as confirmation is an end of every dispute. In the same way God, desiring even more to show to the heirs of the promise the unchangeableness of His purpose, interposed with an oath, so that by two unchangeable things in which it is impossible for God to lie, we who have taken refuge would have strong encouragement to take hold of the hope set before us." ~Hebrews 6:13-18

The key concepts in this passage from Hebrews 6 are that it is impossible for God to lie and there is no one greater than Himself to whom He might lose control and negate the oath as a result. When God made the oath to Abraham, He put His own reputation and power as collateral, not basing it on something or someone He had no control over. In contrast, when we make a commitment or promise to someone, it should be a simple yes or no. To bring an oath into the matter would be a way to set it up for failure.

In the Old Hebrew tradition, there was the law of the vow. This law clarified how vows could be made, kept, and forgiven. For example, if a minor made a vow, the minor could get out of the vow if the parents disapproved of the vow that was made. The parents were to speak up right away to nullify the vow made by a minor child; if nothing was said by the parents, then the vow was to remain intact.

When a married woman made a vow to someone, it would remain binding unless the husband verbally made his disapproval known. Then the woman's vow was nullified and she was not bound by God or man to keep the vow. If the husband did not make his disapproval known, then the woman was bound by her vow.

Vows were usually made as a promise for giving to the Lord in exchange for godly favor. They were normally monetary but in some cases they involved human beings. A good example of a tragic, rash vow was when Jephthah vowed to sacrifice to God the first thing that greeted him from his tent. In his case, it ended up being his daughter.

"Jephthah made a vow to the LORD and said, 'If You will indeed give the sons of Ammon into my hand, then it shall be that whatever comes out of the doors of my house to meet me when I return in peace from the sons of Ammon, it shall be the LORD'S, and I will offer it up as a burnt offering'...When Jephthah came to his house at Mizpah, behold, his daughter was coming out to meet him with tambourines and with dancing. Now she was his one and only child; besides her he had no son or daughter. ... So she said to him, 'My father, you have given your word to the LORD; do to me as you have said, since the LORD has avenged you of your enemies, the sons of Ammon.'... At the end of two months she returned to her father, who did to her according to the vow which he had made; and she had no relations with a man. Thus it became a custom in Israel." ~Judges 11:30-39

Jephthah's vow cost him his only daughter, but I think it is interesting that he told the Lord "whoever" came out of the tent and "I will offer him" as a burnt offering. Usually *whoever* means any person and *him* means a man, but the Bible says Jephthah didn't have any sons. I wonder who was he thinking of when he made this vow to God!

This vow is an example of a rash vow. A rash vow is one that is made without a lot of thought to the promise behind it. Many times this kind of vow has regret attached at the end because of its exaggeration and personal sacrifice of loss. When Herod promised his wife's daughter anything up to "half of the kingdom" for her delightful dancing, he ended up having to give John the Baptist's head on a platter to satisfy her request. "Up to half of the kingdom" is another good example of a rash vow.

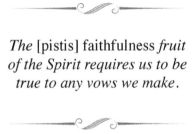

The [pistis] faithfulness *fruit of the Spirit requires us to be true to any vows we make.*

The *[pistis] faithfulness* fruit of the Spirit requires us to be true to any vows we make. Many people make vows to God that might be considered rash. "Lord, if you save my son, I'll go to church every Sunday for the rest of my life." "If you'll bless me with this new job, I'll give you 20 percent of my income instead of 10 percent." Can you think of other rash vows you have made or have heard others make in the past?

The Israelites were not allowed to vow to God anything that belonged to God in the first place such as the tithe, the firstfruits, and the firstborn of the livestock. They were also not allowed to vow those things that were under the ban or any unclean thing. The items under the ban included items that were forbidden by God to have in one's possession. For example, when Joshua took his troops to conquer Jericho, all the possessions in Jericho were under the ban, which meant the Israelites were not allowed to take any of the items in that city as spoil or bounty for their victory.

"Nothing from that which is put under the ban shall cling to your hand, in order that the LORD may turn from His burning anger and show mercy to you, and have compassion on you and make you increase, just as He has sworn to your fathers." ~Deuteronomy 13:17

The Israelites were allowed to vow things that came freely from the heart. When they did so, however, they were required to uphold every promise or vow or there would be stiff penalties and consequences.

"When you make a vow to the LORD your God, you shall not delay to pay it, for it would be sin in you, and the LORD your God will surely require it of you. However, if you refrain from vowing, it would not be sin in you. You shall be careful to perform what goes out from your lips, just as you have voluntarily vowed to the LORD your God, what you have promised." ~Deuteronomy 23:21-23

If an Israelite didn't make a vow to God, that was fine. It would never be held against him. But when a vow was made, the one making the vow was held to the vow and it became a sin if that person was delayed in paying it or disregarded it altogether.

"When you make a vow to God, do not be late in paying it; for He takes no delight in fools. Pay what you vow! It is better that you should not vow than that you should vow and not pay. Do not let your speech cause you to sin and do not say in the presence of the messenger of God that it was a mistake. Why should God be angry on account of your voice and destroy the work of your hands? For in

many dreams and in many words there is emptiness. Rather, fear God." ~Ecclesiastes 5:4-7

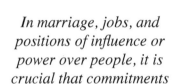

In marriage, jobs, and positions of influence or power over people, it is crucial that commitments be made and kept.

In marriage, jobs, and positions of influence or power over people, it is crucial that commitments be made and kept. God does not require us all to get married. He does not demand that we enter into employment contracts or seek out positions of power and influence such as those in leadership or government. But when we choose to move forward in these directions, then the vows, commitments, and promises that are required of them must be fulfilled without delay and with integrity. If we choose to make them, we can draw upon the character of God in us, the *[pistis] faithfulness* fruit of the Spirit, to fulfill them.

Faithfulness with Possessions

Stewardship is faithfulness with possessions. The principle of stewardship appears in many places in the Old and the New Testaments. God entrusts a person with possessions

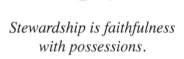

Stewardship is faithfulness with possessions.

and then requires that person to take care of or share those things with others. Learning to give possessions away is also a prevalent theme in the Bible. When we give away to others, God says He will give back to us in even greater proportions.

Finding value in a possession is an issue of the heart and not necessarily the brain. The value you have for something becomes evident and is measured by the degree of ease for you to dispose of it. For instance, I'd have an easier time throwing my plastic ring away, the one I got out of a bubble gum machine, than my wedding ring. I value my diamond and gold more than the plastic. My wedding ring cost me more and has more sentimental properties to it than the plastic ring. Being conscious of this principle of stewardship and acting on it is a way we exercise the *[pistis] faithfulness* fruit of the Spirit in our lives.

Jesus taught in a parable that it is the faithful and sensible slave that the master puts in charge of all of his household and eventually all of his possessions.

"Therefore be on the alert, for you do not know which day your Lord is coming. But be sure of this, that if the head of the house had known at what time of the night the thief was coming, he would have been on the alert and would not have allowed his house to be broken into. For this reason you also must be ready; for the Son of Man is coming at an hour when you do not think He will. Who then is the faithful and sensible slave whom his master put in charge of his household to give them their food at the proper time? Blessed is that slave whom his master finds so doing when he comes. Truly I say to you that he will put him in charge of all his possessions. But if that evil slave says in his heart, 'My master is not coming for a long time,' and begins to beat his fellow slaves and eat and drink with drunkards; the master of that slave will come on a day when he does not expect him and at an hour which he does not know, and will cut him in pieces and assign

him a place with the hypocrites; in that place there will be weeping and gnashing of teeth." ~Matthew 24:42-51

Faithfulness with Provisions

The provisions God gives to us in our lives include money and time, and both give us opportunities to display the *[pistis] faithfulness* fruit of the Spirit. Lately God has given me a greater respect for the value of the small things in my life, especially the value of even the smallest increment of money. This lesson hit home with me a couple of weeks ago when it came to the issue of paying sales tax.

> *The provisions God gives to us in our lives include money and time, and both give us opportunities to display the [pistis] faithfulness fruit of the Spirit.*

My church is a nonprofit corporation that is exempt from sales tax. So when I purchase something for the church, I am very careful to remind the sales clerk of the exempt status. The sales clerk sometimes must recalculate my purchase minus the sales tax. Sometimes I forget to mention the status at the register, and then I end up paying sales tax. I'm getting better at the process.

The Lord was speaking to me the other day that I need to value the small amount that I can save through the tax exemption. Valuing the small money saved would make me a better, faithful steward of the money. Saving 59 cents on an item may not seem like very much, but to the Spirit, not stewarding, or valuing, that small amount would be disregarding the favor the church has with the IRS. It would tell God that I struggle with faithfulness in the small things.

Scripture says it's very important to be faithful and steward the possessions God gives us, even if the possession is favor or savings.

"He who is faithful in a very little thing is faithful also in much; and he who is unrighteous in a very little thing is unrighteous also in much. Therefore if you have not been faithful in the use of unrighteous wealth, who will entrust the true riches to you? And if you have not been faithful in the use of that which is another's, who will give you that which is your own? No servant can serve two masters; for either he will hate the one and love the other, or else he will be devoted to one and despise the other. You cannot serve God and wealth." ~Luke 16:10-14

Being faithful with someone else's money earns you the blessing of increase in your own money. Notice here how God wants to see our faithfulness with "the use of unrighteous" before He trust us with "true riches." There is a separation between what's unrighteous and what's true. If Jesus represents everything that is true and the world represents everything that is unrighteous, then God is watching very carefully to see how faithful we are with the things we are given in the world to determine how much He will give us in Kingdom treasure. He is specific here with wealth and possessions: things and money.

Time, like money, is a commodity. It has been established by God, and we are forced to live within its allowances and restrictions. It is like the waves of the seashore. They are never ending, but once each wave is gone, we can never get it back. Time is fleeting in the same way and yet abundant as long as we have another breath. Though God is not bound by time or ruled by it, He works within the timeframes He's given us. God doesn't need a lot of time to accomplish His works, and He expects us to accomplish our works in the time He's given us.

Many facets of time are mentioned in the Bible, and God requires that we are faithful to each one He gives us. Here are a few.

- Course of time – Genesis 4:3; 2 Chronicles 21:19
- Appointed time – Genesis 18:14; 21:2; Exodus 13:10; 23:15; 34:18; Ecclesiastes 3:1-11
- Definite time – Exodus 9:5
- Loss of time – Exodus 21:19
- Plowing time – Exodus 34:21
- Sowing time – Leviticus 26:5
- Judgment time – 1 Peter 4:17
- Proper time – 1 Peter 5:6
- Short time –Revelation 12:12; 20:3
- Half time – Revelation 12:14

The Bible mentions time as a possession that every emotion, action, and reaction has.

"There is an appointed time for everything. And there is a time for every event under heaven—a time to give birth and a time to die; a time to plant and a time to uproot what is planted. A time to kill and a time to heal; a time to tear down and a time to build up. A time to weep and a time to laugh; a time to mourn and a time to dance. A time to throw stones and a time to gather stones; a time to embrace and a time to shun embracing. A time to search and a time to give up as lost; a time to keep and a time to throw away. A time to tear

apart and a time to sew together; a time to be silent and a time to speak. A time to love and a time to hate; a time for war and a time for peace. What profit is there to the worker from that in which he toils? I have seen the task which God has given the sons of men with which to occupy themselves. He has made everything appropriate in its time. He has also set eternity in their heart, yet so that man will not find out the work which God has done from the beginning even to the end." ~Ecclesiastes 3:1-11

I encourage you to be aware of the *[pistis] faithfulness* fruit of the Spirit in how you value the time given to you by God for family, friends, and appointments as well as time commitments in building, sustaining, and repairing relationships. One thing about time is that we are not guaranteed another minute and yet we are promised eternity, which is passing over from the earthly time zone to the heavenly time zone. There we will live forever through faith in the Son of God, whom God sent to the earth in the "fullness of the time" (Galatians 4:4; Ephesians 1:10).

Time to Pray

If God has spoken to you during this chapter and you desire to have more of God's *[pistis] faithfulness* fruit working in your life, pray this prayer.

"Father in heaven, I want You to show more of Your [pistis] faithfulness fruit in me in regard to my relationships, possessions, provisions, and time. Help me to recognize when I am being unfaithful

to those things You have entrusted to me, and remind me of how faithful You are."

Time to Apply

Take some time and ask God in your *Life Enhancement Journal* at the back of the book, about your amount of *faithfulness* fruit on display in all situations in your life. Be sure not to rush through this exercise because faithfulness is one of God's unchangeable qualities! When you have completed this section of your journal, then turn to Chapter Ten: *Your GENTLENESS Makes Me Great.*

Chapter Ten

Your GENTLENESS Makes Me Great

*G*od has given us furry kittens, fluffy chicks, and fragile baby bunnies as symbols of gentleness in nature. What causes us to associate them with the beautiful character quality we know as gentleness? Perhaps it's what these creatures are not. They are not harsh, mean, and vindictive. There is no guile in their behaviors. They aren't predators looking to kill, maim, mangle, or destroy. Instead, they are innocent, sweet, cute, and pleasant to be around. These characteristics are all part of the *gentleness* fruit of the Spirit.

The *gentleness* fruit of the Spirit in the Bible is the word *praÿtēs* in the Greek, which means to have mildness of disposition, meekness (humility), and consideration. Notice in this passage that gentleness is something we "put on." It's not a natural character quality. It's God's gentleness within us, His fruit of the Spirit, that helps us bear with one another and forgive each other.

"So, as those who have been chosen of God, holy and beloved, put on a heart of compassion, kindness [chrēstotēs], humility, gentleness [praÿtēs] and patience [makrothymia]; bearing with one another, and

forgiving each other, whoever has a complaint against anyone; just as the Lord forgave you, so also should you." ~Colossians 3:12-13 (bracketed text mine)

As disciples of Christ, we are tested in our gentleness when people we encounter act in ways that bring the complaining out in us. In those instances, it's the *[praÿtēs] gentleness* fruit of the Spirit active in our lives that keeps us harmless, considerate, and kind in our actions toward those who act in offensive ways. It's the *[praÿtēs] gentleness* fruit of the Spirit that David referred to in Psalm 18.

"You have also given me the shield of Your salvation, and your right hand upholds me; and Your gentleness ['anavah or praÿtēs] makes me great." ~Psalm 18:35 (bracketed text mine)

God makes us great through the gentleness fruit of the Spirit. What an incredible promise to lay hold of in our lives!

Notice that David speaks of God's gentleness as making him great. The Old Testament Hebrew word`anavah here is the equivalent of the New Testament Greek word *praÿtēs* used for the *gentleness* fruit of the Spirit.

God makes us great through the *gentleness* fruit of the Spirit. What an incredible promise to lay hold of in our lives!

Gentleness Isn't Weakness

Paul the apostle had to address the Corinthian church's issues many times, and the New Testament includes two letters he wrote to the church. His job as the apostle and founder of the faith in their community was to call to light their sins. His first letter seemed to them to be bold with correction and judgment. He wrote the second letter when he realized the Corinthian Christians were getting confused between his boldness in his letters and his gentleness or meekness when he was with them face-to-face. They had begun to see his demeanor and behavior when he was with them as a sign of weakness, and so instead of responding with repentance, they mocked him and disrespected him.

"Now I, Paul, myself urge you by the meekness and gentleness [praÿtēs] of Christ—I who am meek when face to face with you, but bold toward you when absent! I ask that when I am present I need not be bold with the confidence with which I propose to be courageous against some, who regard us as if we walked according to the flesh."
~2 Corinthians 10:1-2 (bracketed text mine)

You've heard the saying, "It's not what you say but how you say it." Well, here the apostle Paul was trying to convince the Corinthians that when he was with them, he intentionally allowed the meekness and gentleness of Christ to govern him as he corrected them and not the harshness and boldness of the flesh.

When you are talking with someone face-to-face, you can say the same straightforward and truthful words that you might write in a letter, but the spirit in which you speak those words can be as Paul describes: in meekness (with humility) and in gentleness (mild and with consideration). If you only write on a piece of paper what you wish to say in strong words and give it without speaking, it will come across in a different light because it will be received without the benefit of body language, voice inflection, gentle or affirming touches, or facial expressions to convey the true spirit behind the words. They will be just words on paper with the interpretation left up to the receiver, and that interpretation will be subject to whatever particular frame of mind the receiver is in on the day the written words are read.

In this passage, we see that Paul wrote out his words of correction, and they apparently came across bold and harsh. Paul knew this, and he felt it necessary to explain the spirit in which he wanted to convey his message and correction, which was in "meekness and gentleness." To make his point clear, he gave the Corinthians a choice as to how they wanted him to speak with them.

"What do you desire? Shall I come to you with a rod, or with love and a spirit of [praÿtēs] gentleness?" ~1 Corinthians 4:21 (bracketed text mine)

Gentleness in Restoration

So often we find ourselves in relationship with people who confess a love for God but end up finding themselves in situations that are very ungodly. They may revert to habits and addictions or become bitter against people they misunderstand or people who have offended them. Greed, lust, adultery, and other forms of immorality may snare them, and they may end up "falling away" from the faith. When any of these things happen, a natural reaction for us is to want to reject them and not use our *gentleness* fruit of the Spirit, thinking that our well-meaning demands and harsh behavior toward them will somehow "snap" them out of it. They'll realize that we mean business and repent of their behavior. While there may be a place for this "disassociation" as a last resort (1 Corinthians 5), it is not appropriate until we have taken many steps to restore them.

"Brethren, even if anyone is caught in any trespass, you who are spiritual, restore such a one in a spirit of [praÿtēs] gentleness; each one looking to yourself, so that you too will not be tempted. ~ Galatians 6:1 (bracketed text mine)

There is a mandate in this verse for how we are to approach restoration. We are to call upon the *gentleness* fruit of the Spirit when dealing with those caught in a trespass. If the kindness of God leads people to repentance, then surely the *[praÿtēs] gentleness* fruit of His people will do the same thing. It's the way of the devil that is harsh, demanding, isolating, and rejecting, not God's. His way is kind, gentle, loving, peaceful, joyful, patient, faithful, and full of self-control. That's how we are to be when dealing with the sinner and the sinning saint. Paul admonishes Titus to remind the church of this truth.

> *We are to call upon the gentleness fruit of the Spirit when dealing with those caught in a trespass.*

"Be subject to the rulers, to the authorities, to be obedient, to be ready for every good deed, to malign no one, to be peaceable, gentle, showing every consideration for all men." ~Titus 3:1-2

The instruction here is to malign "no one" but to be peaceable, *gentle,* and considerate of "all men." "No one" and "all men" include the sinner and the sinning saint alike. Paul goes on to remind Titus of how foolish, disobedient, deceived, and enslaved to various lusts and pleasures all of humankind was at one time, spending their life in malice and envy, hateful, and hating one another; but then the kindness (which includes *gentleness* as a attribute) of God the Savior and His love for humankind appeared and saved them, not because of their deeds, but because of His mercy, His washing, His renewing by the Holy Spirit that He poured out upon us richly through Jesus Christ the Savior at the cross (Titus 3:3-6).

Gentleness in Correcting Opposition

There is a temptation inherent in our zealousness for the gospel of Jesus Christ. In the name of preserving our faith and defending Christianity, we can move into harshness in our reactions to opposition. I've been guilty of doing this so many times, especially with the ones I love the most. Friendly discussions have turned into "knock-out-drag-downs." It's a wonder anyone came out alive when it was over. This behavior was happening with Timothy in his ministry, and we know it because Paul found it necessary to address it in his second letter to him.

"But refuse foolish and ignorant speculations, knowing that they pro-duce quarrels. The Lord's bond-servant must not be quarrelsome, but be kind to all, able to teach, patient when wronged, with [praÿtēs] gentleness correcting those who are in opposition, if perhaps God may grant them repentance leading to the knowledge of the truth, and they may come to their senses and escape from the snare of the

devil, having been held captive by him to do his will." ~*2 Timothy 2:23-26 (bracketed text mine)*

When tempted to quarrel, Timothy was admonished to "be kind to all." He was advised to use the ignorance of others as an opportunity to teach the word of God and educate them in the truth. Timothy had a holy mandate as a minister of the gospel to display the *[makrothymia] patience* fruit of the Spirit when others wronged him. When these situations came about and opposition was against God, His ways, and His people, Timothy was to use his pastoral authority to bring a correction but with the *[praÿtēs] gentleness* fruit of the Spirit. Through this proper pastoral behavior, God would be free to minister to the hardness of men's hearts, grant repentance, and free the rebellious from the devil's grip.

Gentleness is the key to the power that can unlock God's grace in the lives of seeking, confused unbelievers as well as in the lives of contentious, misguided believers. In either case, gentleness paves the way for God to save their souls.

> *Gentleness is the key to the power that can unlock God's grace in the lives of seeking, confused unbelievers as well as in the lives of contentious, misguided believers.*

Time to Pray

If you would like God to help you with the *gentleness* fruit of the Spirit, please take time to pray this prayer.

"Holy Spirit, I need Your gentleness fruit to be released in my heart and life in a greater way. I now understand that it's Your [praÿtēs]

gentleness operating in my heart that will allow the Father to release the disobedient and the wayward into a greater love and commitment to You. I want my actions, both in speech and behavior, to reflect Your mild disposition, humility, and consideration of others. I want to be like Jesus, gentle and lowly of heart; not harsh, biting, and condescending to the ignorant and hurtful ones that wrong me. I understand that I need a greater measure of [praÿtēs] gentleness in my life. Give me grace to display the gentleness fruit in my life. When I am put in a position to bring correction or restoration to others, let me do it in the spirit of [praÿtēs] gentleness so You will grant them repentance and bring them to the truth. I repent and ask You to forgive me for my sins. In Jesus' name, amen."

Time to Apply

It's time to go to the *Life Enhancement Journal* at the back of the book and turn to Chapter Ten. Be sure to pray through the exercise while asking God the questions you may have on the *gentleness* fruit. When you are finished recording your answers, then proceed to Chapter Eleven: *Be Useful: Add to Your Knowledge SELF-CONTROL.*

Chapter Eleven

Be Useful: Add to Your Knowledge
SELF-CONTROL

$\mathcal{I}$ used to wonder why *self-control* was listed last in the nine fruit of the Spirit. Notice its placement in this verse.

"But the fruit of the Spirit is love, joy, peace, patience, kindness, goodness, faithfulness, gentleness, self-control; against such things there is no law." *~Galatians 5:22-23*

After studying this fruit, I came to realize that the lack of the fruit of the Spirit *self-control* in God's people has been a major factor in advancing a tainted reputation of God on the earth. Certain behaviors that stem from the lack of self-control such as drug addictions, sex addictions, food addictions, and gambling and pornography addictions have caused premature deaths, degradation and destruction of the family unit. Battles for gender identity and the widespread spirit of abuse and violence run rampant on the earth due to the lack of the fruit of the Spirit *self-control*. Lack of self-control is now widely accepted inside churches and outside of them because it is culturally accepted as an identity issue in human beings. Have you noted how little is said these days in sermons about the *self-control* fruit of the Spirit?

> *The self-control fruit of the Spirit may be the most challenging fruit to perfect and display in our lives.*

Here is why I think it comes last in the list. The *self-control* fruit of the Spirit may be the most challenging fruit to perfect and display in our lives. It requires believers to die to addictive behaviors that bring overwhelming pleasure and identity to the fleshly man.

The effects of the lack of self-control in addictions such as alcohol, sex, and greed are not necessarily appreciated by the church and the culture, but they are increasingly being accepted by our society as a whole because they are disguised as aspects of personal identity. Possibly saddest of all is the fact that a misunderstanding of the doctrine of God's grace within the church culture has allowed the lack of the *self-control* fruit of the Spirit to be a labeled as normal and accepted.

The Greek word for the fruit *self-control* is *egkrateia,* which is defined as having the virtue of mastering desires and passions, especially one's sensual appetites. I used to think of self-control as simply the ability to delay one's anger or violent reaction by choosing milder

> *The* [egkrateia] self-control *fruit, I now see, is about the ability to control ourselves relative to obsessions, addictions, and passions, both morally and physically.*

responses than ones such as kicking the dog or yelling obscenities in public or in family interactions. The Bible tells us, however, that this sort of restraint in behavior is actually exercising the *patience* fruit of the Spirit, as discussed in Chapter Six. The *[egkrateia] self-control* fruit, I now see, is about the ability to control ourselves relative to obsessions, addictions, and passions, both morally and physically.

In this final chapter, we'll look at the importance of the *[egkrateia] self-control* fruit in decision making, in faith building and usefulness in God's Kingdom, and in spiritual discipline. Then we'll look at the opposite of the *self-control* fruit, which the Bible speaks of as self-indulgence. We'll examine self-indulgence in material possessions and romantic relationships, and then we'll see how self-indulgence and the *self-control* fruit are expected to play out in the end times.

Self-Control in Decision Making

When the apostle Paul was being detained by Governor Felix (see Acts 24), he was able to stand before him and give an account of the righteousness of God and his faith in the resurrection of the dead. Felix was very interested in Paul's testimony until he began to speak of three specific issues, one of them self-control.

"But some days later Felix arrived with Drusilla, his wife who was a Jewess, and sent for Paul and heard him speak about faith in Christ Jesus. But as he was discussing righteousness, [egkrateia] self-control and the judgment to come, Felix became frightened and said, 'Go away for the present, and when I find time I will summon you.'"
~Acts 24:24-25 (bracketed text mine)

We see in this portion of Scripture that as Paul began to share his faith in Jesus Christ, the subjects of righteousness, self-control, and God's judgment came up. I can imagine the conviction of the Holy Spirit coming upon Felix regarding these three subjects in his life: "righteousness" regarding the standard of being right with God, making right decisions in life, and having an upright and blameless heart; "self-control" in dealing with his behavior stemming out of his inability to control his fleshly passions and appetites; and the coming "judgment" for how Felix was choosing to live, the end result being heaven or hell.

The *love, joy,* or *patience* fruit were not at issue here relative to the judgment Felix was to encounter with Jesus Christ. Instead, by mentioning the judgment to come, Paul was illuminating for Felix the importance of the *[egkrateia] self-control* fruit of the Spirit and what a weighty measure of judgment the lack of it would provoke upon him. In response, Felix became frightened and sent Paul away until another time. He had been hoping Paul would pay him off with money (Acts 24:26) in the form of a bribe. When he saw that Paul's *[egkrateia] self-control* fruit of the Spirit (his passions) were in check and were not such that would lead him to bribery for his release, Felix left him in prison for two years (Acts 24:27).

The *self-control* fruit of the Spirit present in Paul and the lack of it in Felix became the catalyst for the decisions Felix made about Paul and his words. If Felix had had the *self-control* fruit working in him, his decisions might have been different. Paul's *self-control* fruit, however, was on display. As a result, he did not give Felix money for his release.

"At the same time too, he was hoping that money would be given him by Paul; therefore he also used to send for him quite often and converse with him. But after two years had passed, Felix was succeeded

by Porcius Festus, and wishing to do the Jews a favor, Felix left Paul imprisoned." ~*Acts 24:26-27*

This story shows that many times there is a worldly price to pay when we are walking in the fruit of the Spirit *self-control*. Paul's *self-control* fruit might have triggered the persecution and imprisonment he received at the hands of Felix. In these times, it is important to remember, as Paul

When the [egkrateia] self-control *fruit of the Spirit is on display in full force in our lives, we are not mastered by our passions and desires.*

did, that we live for life everlasting and not for this temporary life. When the *[egkrateia]self-control* fruit of the Spirit is on display in full force in our lives, we are not mastered by our passions and desires. We have control over the parts of ourselves that are indulgent or focused on serving our fleshly needs.

Self-Control in Faith Building and Usefulness

The self-control *fruit is a quality in our life that can build our faith, keep us loving others, and help us see the need to forgive.*

The *self-control* fruit is a quality in our life that can build our faith, keep us loving others, and help us see the need to forgive. In a nutshell, it makes us useful in many ways to God on this earth, and the lack of it simply hinders our usefulness to God. As the apostle Peter said in his second epistle, if *[egkrateia] self-control* fruit is present and increasing, it will render us both useful and fruitful to God.

"Now for this very reason also, applying all diligence, in your faith supply moral excellence, and in your moral excellence, knowledge, and in your knowledge, [egkrateia] self-control, and in your [egkrateia] self-control, perseverance, and in your perseverance, godliness, and in your godliness, brotherly kindness, and in your brotherly kindness, love. For if these qualities are yours and are increasing, they render you neither useless nor unfruitful in the true knowledge of our Lord Jesus Christ. For he who lacks these qualities is blind or short-sighted, having forgotten his purification from his former sins. ~2 Peter 1:5-9 (bracketed text mine)

The apostle Paul indicates here that the *self-control* fruit of the Spirit is a quality of character in life that needs to be pursued, or obtained by "applying all diligence." Lacking self-control, or lacking the virtue of one who masters his desires and passions, especially his sensual appetites, is a sure potion for a life disaster. Saying so may seem harsh, but the Bible is very clear in this verse that without the *[egkrateia] self-control* fruit of the Spirit, we remain blinded and at best shortsighted.

We, because of human nature, are constantly forgetting how much we've been forgiven for our sins and needing to be reminded of it. When we forget how much we've been forgiven, we live in the torment of guilt and shame. Hurt people hurt people. Unforgiven people do not forgive other people. In other words, the pain that comes from forgetting how much we have been forgiven, combined with our weakness in displaying the *[egkrateia] self-control* fruit, causes us to bring pain to others. Also, when we are unaware of how much we've been forgiven by God, we are unaware of our need to forgive others. The significance of the blood of Christ and His forgiveness is diminished to a past experience when we first prayed to be forgiven. For this reason, the Bible is clear in 2 Peter 1:5-8 that unless we *continually* practice attributes of God's character including *[egkrateia]* self-control, we become useless to God because our consciences are tormented with our lack of power in our life to overcome our passions. Aggressively going after the *[egkrateia] self-control* fruit of the Spirit in our lives advances us on the track of victory, developing deeper spiritual discipline and greater levels of love and forgiveness for others.

Self-Control in Spiritual Discipline

In my life, I have many personal disciplines that have helped me achieve high honors from mankind. As I shared in earlier chapters, I grew up with horses. At a very young age, I began showing horses in equestrian riding, halter, jumping, and trail skills. I perfected the discipline of riding my horse every day and learned how to train my horse to follow my commands. My personal discipline in this area of my life has paid off throughout the years. I have amassed blue ribbons, trophies, and championship plaques that are stored in boxes, taking up space in my garage.

As a teenager I joined the high school song-leading squad and was required to attend many strenuous practices, watch my diet, and dress and act a certain way to maintain my prestigious status. We competed in many song-leading competitions and won some beautiful trophies that are displayed in my trophy case to this day.

As a young adult in my 20s, I ran and competed in 5k and 10k races. The training was hard and included early morning runs, diet restrictions, and water and sleep demands. These personal disciplines did not come easy nor did they ever come natural for me, but I took them seriously and became very good at what I did. Though I never became a champion or ever had the drive to compete in the Olympics, I enjoyed long distance running and found great pleasure in the payoff of the health and beauty benefits that accompanied it.

In 1 Corinthians, Paul talks about "running a race to win." The personal discipline that is needed to achieve a perishable wreath is minor compared to the spiritual discipline of the *[egkrateia] self-control* fruit of the Spirit that lead us to inherit the imperishable wreath of eternal life.

"Do you not know that those who run in a race all run, but only one receives the prize? Run in such a way that you may win. Everyone who competes in the games exercises [egkrateia] self-control in all things. They then do it to receive a perishable wreath, but we an imperishable. Therefore I run in such a way, as not without aim; I box in such a way, as not beating the air; but I discipline my body and make it my slave, so that, after I have preached to others, I myself will not be disqualified." ~1 Corinthians 9:24-27 (bracketed text mine)

Paul likened the Christian life to a race and said he knew that he too could be disqualified if he didn't exercise the [egkrateia] self-control *fruit of the Spirit.*

The apostle Paul understood the self-control needed to compete in any game. In this case, Paul likened the Christian life to a race and said he knew that he too could be disqualified if he didn't exercise the *[egkrateia] self-control* fruit of the Spirit. It's one thing to talk about it or write about it, but it's another thing to live it. He knew that without the *[egkrateia] self-control* fruit in his life, his lustful and animal-like passions, left unchecked by the Holy Spirit, would disqualify him from entering the Kingdom he was so committed to promoting. The *[egkrateia] self-control* fruit of the Spirit, he declared, was the determining factor in the end that would qualify or disqualify him.

Self-Indulgence in Hypocrisy

There's another word used in the Bible in passages talking about the need for self-control, and it's the opposite of the fruit of the Spirit. The word is *akrasia*, which is defined in *Strong's Concordance* as being in want of self-control, incontinence, intemperance. Most of us probably think of *incontinence* as a physical condition, but its definition also includes the failure to restrain sexual appetite. The word *intemperance* we understand as the lack of moderation, especially with regard to habitual or excessive drinking of intoxicants. The definitions of these two words show some of the outcomes of the lack of the *self-control* fruit.

Another word for the lack of the *self-control* fruit is *self-indulgence*. The word *self-indulgence* is defined as excessive or unrestrained gratification of one's own appetites and desires. The Bible warns against self-indulgence. Jesus is very clear at the end of all the "woes" about what happens to people that live a life of self-indulgence with no regard to *[egkrateia] self-control*.

"Woe to you, scribes and Pharisees, hypocrites! For you clean the outside of the cup and of the dish, but inside they are full of robbery and self-indulgence." ~Matthew 23:25

"You serpents, you brood of vipers, how will you escape the sentence of hell?" ~Matthew 23:33

Jesus was really good at reading the hearts of men and women. He saw that some of the religious leaders of the day placed a lot of importance on what things looked like on the outside to others looking on. The impression that they wanted to portray to those observing them and the pious reputation they wanted to uphold meant more to them than the *[egkrateia] self-control* fruit of the Spirit in their lives. Here is Jesus' warning, in my words:

> Be wary of your judgment to come, you scribes and Pharisees, you who claim or pretend to have certain beliefs about what is right but who behave in a way that disagrees with those beliefs. You make sure what man sees on the outside of your important life is holy and blameless, but I know that inside your heart you are full of covetousness, wanting things you can't have. You have a desire to take from others and benefit yourselves, and all you care about is satisfying your sexual desires in the most perverse way along with the unruly passions of the flesh that rule your behavior, making sure you're only satisfying yourselves.

Wow. No wonder Jesus was not their favorite person! He saw that they did not have the *[egkrateia] self-control* fruit of the Spirit, and this opposition of the Spirit's character classified them as hypocrites, worthy of rebuke, and living without the true God in their lives or the life to come.

God is looking for His people to display to the world *[egkrateia] self-control* fruit of the Spirit in all avenues of life with no hypocrisy. Saying we follow God but live in self-indulgence is a hypocritical act and will receive rebuke in the same way the scribes and Pharisees experienced rebuke from Jesus.

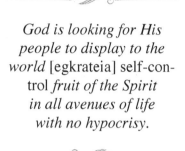

God is looking for His people to display to the world [egkrateia] self-control *fruit of the Spirit in all avenues of life with no hypocrisy.*

Self-Control in the Marriage Relationship

Self-control and the opposite of it, self-indulgence, are also discussed in the Scriptures as they apply to personal relationships. *Self-control* fruit of the Spirit in relationships is a vital part of fulfilling the will of God in the Christian life. It is so dear to God's heart that He addresses it in the relationship between the husband and wife in the marriage regarding sexual intercourse. He gives clear instruction, through the apostle Paul in his letter to the Corinthian church, that withholding the union of sexual intercourse for any other reason than mutual consent in the areas of fasting and prayer would be equivalent to creating a playground in a couple's relationship for the devil to romp. Withholding or depriving each other of the act of sexual intercourse for selfish reasons would trigger

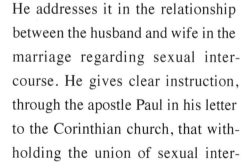

Self-control fruit of the Spirit in relationships is a vital part of fulfilling the will of God in the Christian life.

a temptation for sexual pleasure (self-indulgence) in other areas, which is the opposite of the *[egkrateia] self-control* fruit of the Spirit.

"Stop depriving one another, except by agreement for a time, so that you may devote yourselves to prayer, and come together again so that Satan will not tempt you because of your lack of [egkrateia] self-control. But this I say by way of concession, not of command. Yet I wish that all men were even as I myself am. However, each man has his own gift from God, one in this manner, and another in that." ~*1 Corinthians 7:5-7 (bracketed text mine)*

Pornography, adultery, fornication, prostitution, bestiality, sexual child abuse, rape, and any other form of sexual deviation from what God originally designed in the garden of Eden with Adam and Eve as the model of God's design in relationship are all displays of self-indulgence as a result of a lack of the *[egkrateia] self-control* fruit of the Spirit.

Lack of Self-Control: Signature of the End

As I continue to live my life on this earth, more and more I see the lives of others, including believers, filled with evidence of the lack of self-control. As I said at the beginning of this chapter, I also see their way of life is being considered normal. Television sit-coms are now portraying drug addiction, obesity, and sexual perversions as accepted and sometimes celebrated parts of our culture. Our government is passing laws that legalize known hallucinogenic drugs and diverse sexual orientations as things to be embraced.

I entered the Christian faith at age eighteen, and I have been taking an active part in the fellowship and the gathering of believers ever since. In all these years, I have yet to hear a teaching or an admonition addressing the perils of the lack of the *[egkrateia]* self-control fruit in the lives of believers. As I read through the Bible again and again, I see that the lack of self-control is addressed quite fervently. In fact, it is the lack of this fruit of the Spirit in our culture that is prophesied by the apostle Paul to be a signature sign of the end times, described as "the last days," that Jesus talked about throughout His ministry on the earth.

"But realize this, that in the last days difficult times will come. For men will be lovers of self, lovers of money, boastful, arrogant, revilers, disobedient to parents, ungrateful, unholy, unloving, irreconcilable, malicious gossips, without [egkrateia] self-control, brutal, haters of good, treacherous, reckless, conceited, lovers of pleasure rather than lovers of God, holding to a form of godliness, although they have denied its power; Avoid such men as these." ~2 Timothy 3:1-5 (bracketed text mine)

In this epistle, Paul warns Timothy that the signs of the coming of the Lord will be evident by the following:

- Mankind will experience difficult times (*hard to do, take, or bear; troublesome*).
- Mankind will love themselves (*too intent on one's interests*).
- Mankind will love money (*a strong desire to have or get money, insatiable*).

213

- Mankind will be exceedingly <u>boastful and arrogant</u> (*claiming to have rights*).

- Mankind will be <u>revilers</u> (*speaking evil, slanderous, reproachful, railing, abusive*).

- Mankind will be <u>disobedient</u> to parents (*not persuadable, stubborn, and disobedient*).

- Mankind will be <u>ungrateful</u> (*ungracious, not courteous*).

- Mankind will be <u>unholy</u> (*feeling or showing a lack of respect for God, wicked*).

- Mankind will be <u>unloving</u> (*without natural affection, unsociable, inhuman*).

- Mankind will be <u>irreconcilable</u> (*without treaty or covenant, unable to enter into agreement*).

- Mankind will be <u>malicious gossips</u> (*utterer of false accusations, slanderer, one who tears*).

- Mankind will be <u>*without self-control*</u> (*intemperate, extreme conditions, too much*).

- Mankind will be <u>brutal</u> (*no restraints, savage, fierce*).

- Mankind will be <u>haters of good</u> (*opposed to goodness*).

- Mankind will be <u>treacherous</u> (*betrayer or traitor, committer of treason, untrustworthy*).

- Mankind will be <u>reckless</u> (*fall headlong, sloping precipitously, steep and sudden*).

- Mankind will be <u>conceited</u> (*puffed up with haughtiness and pride, raise like smoke*).

- Mankind will be <u>lovers of pleasure</u> rather than God (*feelings of enjoyment, satisfaction*).

- Mankind will <u>hold a form of godliness</u> (*wearing a sense of a shape that looks holy*).

- Mankind will <u>deny the power of God</u> *(disregard God's interests to display miracles).*

The admonition in verse 5 that accompanies this description is to AVOID all who show evidence of this lack of *[egkrateia] self-control* fruit or participate in such behavior. When the *self-control* fruit of the Spirit is displayed and actively applied in relationships, the Bible says these relationships will grow and prosper. The Bible admonishes Christians to avoid relationships with people that live a life evidenced by the lack of the *self-control* fruit. A

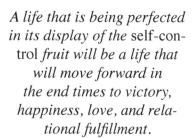

A life that is being perfected in its display of the self-control *fruit will be a life that will move forward in the end times to victory, happiness, love, and relational fulfillment.*

life that is being perfected in its display of the *self-control* fruit will be a life that will move forward in the end times to victory, happiness, love, and relational fulfillment.

If you find yourself lacking in any of these areas or know that there is a great need for the Holy Spirit *[egkrateia] self-control* fruit to be displayed in your life, it's important that you confess the lack to God and call upon the Holy Spirit for His radical power to be released in you. If you are addicted in any way to any behavior that strips you of your ability to be self-governed or regulated by personal and spiritual discipline, now is the time to cry out to God for forgiveness, deliverance, and a new start to have the Holy Spirit manifest His character quality of *[egkrateia] self-control* fruit in your life.

Time to Pray

If God has spoken to you during this chapter and you desire to have more of the *[egkrateia] self-control* fruit of the Spirit working in your life, pray this prayer from your heart.

"Dear Jesus, thank you that You have shined Your light upon my life and shown me where I need the Holy Spirit [egkrateia] self-control fruit in greater measure in my life. I submit my addictions to You and ask You to come into my life and break off the powers that are influencing me to sin against You. Fill me with Your Holy Spirit, and break the chains in my life that keep me bound to any excessive, hurtful, and destructive behavior. In Jesus' name, amen."

Time to Apply

Take some time and ask God in your *Life Enhancement Journal* at the back of the book, about your display of the *[egkrateia] self-control* fruit in all situations in your life. Be sure not to rush through this exercise because the *self-control* fruit is one of God's requirements to live a victorious life!

About the Author

*W*endi Moen is the Co-Pastor and founder of River Rock Christian Fellowship in 2003, the Outpouring School of Ministry in 2008, and P4Npassions4nations world missions network in 2009.

She lives in Reno, Nevada and has been in the ministry with her husband, Eric, since 1986. Wendi and Eric have one son, Robbie, who loves the Lord and graduated from a Bible college in 2011 with a communications degree. He works in broadcasting and the film industry in television.

Wendi has raised up many teachers in the body of Christ to impart the power and presence of God in the lives of their students. P4Npassions4nations world missions network is her latest establishment and has been in full operation since 2009. This missions network ordains, trains, and equips missionaries to go into the nations to win the lost and disciple pastors and leaders.

Wendi has traveled to and ministered in over twenty nations, which includes states and nations in North and South America, Africa, India, China, Nepal, Virgin Islands, Europe, Mexico, the Middle East, Philppines, and many parts of Southeast Asia. Wendi's greatest passion is to watch the power of God work in people's lives, healing the sick and setting them free from their old ways of life into the newness of God's love.

Going After the Good Fruit
Wendi Moen

Life Enhancement Journal
Personal & Group Study Guide

Chapter One
Move in the Gifts and Measure the Fruit

Reflections

1. In Matthew 7:16-23, how did Jesus say that we would be able to recognize the false from the true?

2. In Matthew 7:16-23, what was Jesus referring too?

3. The word "fruit" here in Matthew 7:16-23 is the same word used in the passage on the "fruit of the Spirit" in Galatians 5:22-23. Write out the list of the fruit of the Spirit in Galatians 5:22-23.

_____   _____   _____

_____   _____   _____

_____   _____   _____

4. How do the gifts of the Spirit and the fruit of the Spirit work together?

Your Thoughts

After reading Chapter One, *"Move in the Gifts and Measure the Fruit,"* write down any new revelation that changed your thinking about the importance of the fruit of the Spirit in your life.

God's Thoughts

Ask God how He feels about the display of the fruit of the Spirit in your life.Write down what you hear Him say or what He shows you.

Your Prayer

Write down what you would you like to say to God about your progress in developing the fruit of the Spirit in your life.

Chapter Two
Consider the Fruit Tree

Reflections

1. In my testimony, the Lord used my experience with the cherry tree to show me how I need to "go after" the hard-to-reach fruit of the Spirit in my life. We all have areas in our lives where the fruit of the Spirit are harder to display than others, especially in the times of conflict. What fruit of the Spirit are easier and harder to display in your life in times of conflict?

Fruit easier to display:

Fruit harder to display:

2. Why do you think so many songs have lyrics that center on the fruit of the Spirit?

3. Write out and memorize Galatians 5:22-23. Pick someone in your Bible study group or someone in your sphere of influence to whom you can quote this passage.

Your Thoughts

After reading Chapter Two, *"Consider the Fruit Tree,"* write down a few thoughts that God spoke to you and changed your thinking about on the concept of aggressively going after the fruit of the Spirit.

God's Thoughts

Take the time to ask God which one of the fruit of the Spirit He'd like you to aggressively go after and apply to your life in a greater measure this week. Write down what He tells or shows you.

Your Prayer

Write down your prayer to God regarding the fruit of the Spirit He'd like you to focus on and put on display in a greater measure this week. Keep in mind, many times it takes a conflict to release the fruit of the Spirit in our lives.

Chapter Three

God Is LOVE

Reflections

1. What is the difference between the fruit of the Spirit *[agape] love* and the love the world has?

2. In 1 John 4:7-12, how does the fruit of the Spirit, *[agape] love* define our relationship with God and one another?

3. In 1 Corinthians, 13:4-8, what does it look like when you are displaying the fruit of the Spirit *[agape] love*?

4. Write out and memorize 1 Corinthians 13:4-8 this week. Be ready to quote it in your Bible study group or to someone you love and trust.

Your Thoughts

After reading Chapter Three, *"God Is LOVE,"* write down a few thoughts that God spoke to you and changed your thinking about on the fruit of the Spirit *[agape] love*.

God's Thoughts

Ask God how you can show *[agape] love* fruit this week to someone that you are in conflict with at home, in your job, at school or in your sphere of influence. Write down what He tells you or shows you.

Your Prayer

Write down your prayer to God regarding His thoughts that He revealed to you about exercising the fruit of the Spirit *[agape] love* in your conflicts this week.

Chapter Four

The JOY of the Lord Is Your Strength

Reflections

1. What situations in your life have stolen your *[chara] joy* fruit?

2. In Hebrews 12:1-2, what was it that kept Jesus enduring the painful mission of the cross?

3. In John 16:6-7 and 22, what promise did Jesus make to us?

4. Why does James 1:2-4 tell us to consider or have *[chara] joy* fruit in our trials?

Your Thoughts

After reading Chapter Four, "*The JOY of the Lord Is Your Strength,*" write down the new revelation you received regarding the fruit of the Spirit *[chara] joy.*

God's Thoughts

Ask God what He thinks about the power of *[chara] joy* fruit in your life, especially in the trials that you are going through right now. Write down what you hear Him say or what He shows you.

Your Prayer

Write down your prayer to God regarding His thoughts that He revealed to you regarding exercising the fruit of the Spirit *[chara] joy* in your conflicts this week.

Chapter Five

The PEACE of God Passes Understanding

Reflections

1. Write out the definition of God's fruit of the Spirit *[eirene] peace*.

2. In Matthew 10:34-36, what did Jesus say about His role in coming to the earth? How does *[eirene] peace* fit into His mission?

3. How does *[eirene] peace* fruit in John 16:33 distinguish fear?

4. In Philippians 4:6-8, how does *[eirene] peace* fruit protect the mind?

Your Thoughts

After reading Chapter Five, *"The PEACE of God Passes Understanding,"* write down the new revelation you received regarding the fruit of the Spirit *[eirene] peace.*

God's Thoughts

Ask God His thoughts about the level of *[eirene] peace* fruit that is in in your life. Write down what He tells or shows you.

Your Prayer

Write down your prayer to God regarding the activation of a greater level of *[eirene] peace* fruit in your life.

Chapter Six

Let Your PATIENCE Be Known to Man

Reflections

1. The fruit of the Spirit *[makrothymia] patience* can also be defined with what other words?

2. In Romans 5:1-5, how does the fruit of the Spirit *[makrothymia] patience* or "perseverance" play in the reasons for our tribulations?

3. In Luke 21:16-19, how does *[makrothymia] patience* or "endurance" affect our lives?

4. How can you relate my vision of riding my bike in the sand to how God is perfecting *[makrothymia] patience* fruit, perseverance and endurance, in your life?

Your Thoughts

After reading Chapter Six, "*Let your PATIENCE Be Known to Man,*" write down the new revelation you received regarding the fruit of the Spirit *[makrothymia] patience.*

God's Thoughts

Ask God His thoughts about His desire to perfect the fruit of the Spirit *[makrothymia] patience* in your life. Write down what He tells or shows you.

Your Prayer

Write down your prayer to God regarding the activation of a greater level of *[makrothymia] patience* fruit in your life.

Chapter Seven

The KINDNESS of God Leads to Repentance

Reflections

1. What is your perception of the power of the fruit of the Spirit *[chrēstotēs] kindness?*

2. What does Luke 6:35 say about the fruit of the Spirit *[chrēstotēs] kindness?*

3. In my "One Thin Dime" vision, God melted my hard heart with His *[chrēstotēs] kindness*. Write down a time when God's kindness softened your heart and brought you closer to Him.

4. What does Colossians 3:12-13 tell us to do with the fruit of the Spirit *[chrēstotēs] kindness?* How would this fruit look in full display in your life?

Your Thoughts

After reading Chapter Seven, *"The KINDNESS of God Leads to Repentance,"* write down how your outlook on *[chrēstotēs] kindness* fruit has been changed or enhanced.

God's Thoughts

Ask God what it would look like if the fruit of the Spirit *[chrēstotēs]* kindness were displayed in a greater way in your life.

Your Prayer

Write down your prayer to God regarding your need to display the *kindness* fruit in greater measure in your life.

Chapter Eight

Surely GOODNESS and Mercy Will Follow Me

Reflections

1. What are the similarities and differences between *[agathōsynē]* *goodness* and *[chrēstotēs] kindness* fruit?

   Similarities:

   Differences:

2. What does 2 Thessalonians 1:11-12 say about *[agathōsynē] goodness* fruit and works of faith?

3. Why would it be important to have the fruit of the Spirit *[agathōsynē] goodness* fruit working in your life when you are in a position of admonishing others (Romans 15:14)?

4. How did "Little Miss Goody Two Shoes" get her name? Write down a situation where goodness brought on persecution and blessing in your life.

Your Thoughts

After reading Chapter Eight, *"Surely GOODNESS and Mercy Shall Follow Me,"* write down the new revelation you received regarding the fruit of the Spirit *[agathōsynē] goodness.*

God's Thoughts

Ask God what He thinks about the fruit of the Spirit *[agathōsynē] goodness* that's on display in your life. Write down what you hear Him tell or show you.

Your Prayer

Write down your prayer to God regarding His thoughts that He revealed to you about displaying the fruit of the Spirit *[agathōsynē] goodness.*

Chapter Nine

Your FAITHFULNESS Reaches to the Sky

Reflections

1. Write down an example where the *[pistis] faithfulness* of a friend, co-worker, or family member earned your trust and endeared you to the person in a greater way.

2. In Matthew 23:23, Jesus refers to the fruit of the Spirit *[pistis] faithfulness* as the "weightier" provision of the law. Explain why Jesus would see it this way.

3. What does 1 Peter 4:14-19 tell us about the role of our Creator in times of tribulation and suffering related to His *[pistis] faithfulness*?

4. Why does Jesus warn against making oaths or vows, and how does this warning relates to the *[pisits] faithfulness* fruit?

Your Thoughts

After reading Chapter Nine, "*Your FAITHFULNESS Reaches to the Sky*," write down some key points that you learned about the fruit of the Spirit *[pistis] faithfulness.*

God's Thoughts

Ask God how He feels about the display of the fruit of the Spirit *[pistis] faithfulness* in your life. Write down what you hear Him tell or show you.

Your Prayer

Write down what you would you like to say to God about your growth in *[pistis] faithfulness.*

Chapter Ten

Your GENTLENESS Makes Me Great

Reflections

1. In Colossians 3:12-13, what are we told to do with the fruit of the Spirit *[praÿtēs] gentleness*? What other fruit of the Spirit are working with *gentleness* in this passage, and what are the manifestations?

2. According to Titus 3:1-2, what are the other areas of life that we are admonished to live by the fruit of the Spirit *[praÿtēs] gentleness*?

3. In 2 Timothy 2:22-26, we see when *[praÿtēs] gentleness* fruit is vitally needed. Write down a time when you witnessed and used the fruit of the Spirit *gentleness* to help you in a difficult situation of correction.

4. Write down a time when you wished that a friend, family member, boss, or co-worker would have acted with *gentleness* towards you.

Your Thoughts

After reading Chapter Ten, *"Your GENTLENESS Makes Me Great,"* write down the things you learned about the importance of growing in the fruit of the Spirit *[praÿtēs] gentleness*

God's Thoughts

Take the time to ask God about the areas of your life where you can grow in the fruit of the Spirit *[praÿtēs] gentleness*. Write down what you hear Him tell or show you.

Your Prayer

Write down your prayer to God regarding your need to grow in the fruit of the Spirit *[praÿtēs] gentleness*.

Chapter Eleven

Be Useful: Add to Your Knowledge SELF-CONTROL

Reflections

1. Why do you think Felix became frightened when Paul the Apostle began talking to him about the fruit of the Spirit *[egkrateia] self-control?*

2. How did the fruit of the Spirit *[egkrateia] self-control* help Paul in his interaction with Felix when he was in prison (Acts 24:26-27)?

3. What role does *[egkrateia] self-control* fruit play in 2 Peter 1:5-9? What other fruit of the Spirit are mentioned with *[egkrateia] self-control* that also play into this concept of "usefulness" to God?

4. How does *[egkrateia] self-control* fruit help us finish and win the "race" towards eternal life (1 Corinthians 9:24-27)?

Your Thoughts

After reading Chapter Eleven, *"Be Useful: Add to Your Knowledge SELF-CONTROL,"* write down some new revelation that you received regarding the need for more of the fruit of the Spirit *[egkrateia] self-control.*

God's Thoughts

Ask God what areas in your life should grow in the display of the *[egkrateia] self-control* fruit. Write down what He tells or shows you.

Your Prayer

Write down your *prayer* to God regarding His thoughts on your need to display more fruit of the Spirit *[egkrateia] self-control.*

NOTES